Contributions to Management Science

For further volumes:
http://www.springer.com/series/1505

Sinan Ünsar

Leadership and Communication

A Case from Glass, Textile and Apparel Sector in Turkey

 Springer

Sinan Ünsar
Faculty of Economics and Admin. Sc.
Department of Business Administration
Trakya University
Edirne
Turkey

This book was supported by the Scientific Research Projects of Trakya University

ISSN 1431-1941   ISSN 2197-716X (electronic)
ISBN 978-3-319-05247-2   ISBN 978-3-319-05248-9 (eBook)
DOI 10.1007/978-3-319-05248-9
Springer Cham Heidelberg New York Dordrecht London

Library of Congress Control Number: 2014938998

Printed on acid-free paper

Springer is part of Springer Science+Business Media (www.springer.com)

Preface

The concepts of leadership and communication can be considered as the most dynamic two concepts of organizational behavior. These two concepts can be regarded as the two sides of a coin. Leaders motivate their followers by effectively using communication process. Thus, communication is an indispensable element of leadership.

Leadership is present both at group and enterprise level. Groups and enterprises can achieve their goals thanks to their leaders. The enterprises become successful thanks to their leaders and make a difference from other enterprises. Success and effectiveness of enterprises in today's globalizing world depends on the potential of their leaders. Since majority of enterprises understood the importance and power of leadership, they make their managers or manager candidates to receive leadership training and thus contribute to the leadership development.

On the other hand, it can be stated that the leaders who use and manage communication well become more successful. It can be stated that the leaders who accurately and appropriately explain group members what they should do will be successful. It can be stated that the leaders who recognize their members thanks to communication process will assign tasks to appropriate and correct people.

A review of the literature revealed that interaction between leadership and communication has not been studied much in Turkey. As a result, it can be stated that this book, although partially, will contribute to the related literature.

In this book, the concepts of leadership and communication were tried to be explained through literature knowledge. Definitions and models about the concepts were explained. An empirical study was carried out on employees working in glass, textile, and apparel sectors. The aim of the study was to determine the views of the employees working in the mentioned sectors on leadership behavior types and the method of establishing communication of their manager.

Edirne, Turkey
November 2013

Agah Sinan Ünsar

Introduction

Leadership is one of the most important concepts of today. Considering that there is a managed group and managers both in societies and enterprises, it is observed that leadership, which is one of the most important elements of management, gains prominence. Like in every era, humans always needed and will need a leader when they come together. The method of managing humans in an effective and efficient manner depends on leadership process. Groups and societies feel secure thanks to their leaders, and thus they become more successful. A leader enables communities to follow the right path confidently and safely. In addition, the efforts of the leader to establish and shape future are of great importance.

It may be said that the concept of leadership is as old as history of humanity. After mankind and groups and societies of mankind showed up, the need to affect and lead these masses arose, as well. In the places where societies or groups live, it is needed to leaders who will lead the individuals to certain purposes and aims. The need for effective leaders is increasing day by day in economic, social, political, and business world. Major leaders play such a significant role in business world that they could make a firm, which was on the brink of bankruptcy or went on bankrupt, one of the leading firms of the sector. When the groups are not diverted to a certain place, the power and energy of the group is wasted. Therefore, leaders are the individuals who lead the energy of the groups consisting of people in line with certain ambitions. Individuals in some group are ordinary people, and they do not draw any attention while some individuals affect other people with their character-istics in such a way that they come out as the leader of that group. Moreover, leaders can be seen as individuals who raise awareness about the features of conditions on which their subordinates take place and these leaders lead the subordinates in which way they should act.

Today, leadership is such a popular concept that lots of studies are being carried out, conferences are being held, articles are being written, books are being issued, and institutes are being established about this concept. Thus, it is tried to enlighten the structure and context of leadership much more and put forth its unknown aspects. Furthermore, teachable aspect of leadership is being established in academic sense, as well. On the other hand, there is a comprehensive literature regarding this topic.

Every individual may possess the potential of a leader. However, there is a difference between possessing it and revealing it. It can be said that leadership is an innate feature and it can be developed through training and teaching. For instance, a person who does not have a fine ear for music probably will not be able to play the violin perfectly no matter how much violin lesson he/she takes. Similarly, a person who does not possess the leadership trait will not be able to be a real leader no matter how much he/she gets training and teaching. Therefore, it can be stated that leadership is based on the artistic aspect and is developed with academic support.

Leadership is a social process. It necessitates communication and interaction with people and groups. The leader starts to be shaped and determined after people and group members realize each other. Leaders play significant roles in the amendment and development of especially societies and establishments. Therefore, leadership has a social mission, as well. It can be evaluated that the biggest dream of leaders is to move a society or an establishment to better places.

When it is considered that communication starts after two individuals realize each other, it is seen that this concept is also as old as history of humanity. It can be said that the communication from past to present has undergone radical changes only structurally. Communication is an indispensable process both in society and group life.

Communication plays a crucial role in the whole coordination of departments in establishments so as to reach their purposes. The world has turned into a small village thanks to the radical changes in communication technology. An event occurring at any place of the world can be heard in 10–15 min by the other countries. Thus, communication technology proceeds at an unprecedented pace. As a result, establishments and leaders benefit from this technology, as well.

Leaders should establish good communication with their subordinates in order to be effective. Actually, the success of a leader is related with the quality of communication process he/she establishes with his/her subordinates. A leader who effectively imposes the purposes or targets of the establishment to them and who always communicates with them during the process of application shall be successful. Therefore, those leaders who choose correct communication channel and use it rationally may gain major advantages. On the other hand, it can be said that leaders possessing the ability of establishing correct communication with people can be more successful in affecting people. Basic communication process is highly significant in motivating them and determining their problems.

In line with the above-mentioned evaluations, it was basically dealt with the concepts of leadership and communication in this study. Within this scope, leadership and communication role and importance were explained in order to put forth context framework of the topic at first. Then, leadership theories and communication models were specified. The interaction of leadership and communication was examined through explaining organizational communication and its tools. Consequently, leadership behavior types and communication skills of administrators of the employees working in glass, textile, and confection sectors were determined and the relationship between socio-demographic variables of employees and leadership behavior types and communication forms of the administrators were examined.

Acknowledgments

In loving memory of my beloved parents, Mrs. Maide Unsar and Mr. Arif Unsar, who raised me and put a great effort in my present position...

I would like to thank my invaluable wife Assoc. Prof. Serap Unsar and my dearest daughter Selin who supported and helped me a lot in the period of writing this book. I would also like to thank and present my respect to Associate Prof. Dr. Adil Oğuzhan, who conducted the statistics in the research section of the book and who helped me by contributing with his invaluable knowledge and comments. Also I would like to thank my student, Teaching Assistant Olgun Irmak Çetin, who prepared the graphic design of the book. In addition, I would like to thank my postgraduate students Derya Dinçer and Ferhan Demir who helped me with the organization of statements of the book. Additionally, I would like to thank my colleagues Prof. Dr. Kıymet Çalıyurt and Sam Idowu who encouraged me to publish this book and helped me in editing.

I believe that it will be very beneficial to improve this book if the readers let me know about the mistakes or deficiencies that I might have made while writing the book. I hope this work will be beneficial to the academic field.

Agah Sinan Ünsar

 http://www.igongfesr.org

Contents

List of Figures

List of Graphs

List of Tables

About The Author

Agah Sinan Ünsar was born in Kırklareli, Turkey, in 1967. He received primary and secondary education in Edirne. He graduated from Edirne High School in 1984. He graduated from the Department of Business Management at Open Education Faculty at Eskişehir Anadolu University with a good degree in 1990. He completed his military service as reserve office in 1992. He received master's degree from the department of Business Administration at Institute of Social Sciences of Trakya University and Doctorate degree from the Department of Human Resources Management at Institute of Social Sciences of Istanbul University. He worked in Trakya University as contracted civil servant between the years of 1992–1994. Between 1994 and 1998, he worked as a civil servant in Institute of Social Sciences at Trakya University. He worked as a faculty member in department of Business Administration at Faculty of Economics and Administrative Sciences at Trakya University between 1998 and 2004 and as Assistant Professor between 2004 and 2010. He received Associate Professor degree in the field of "Management and Organization" in 2010. He continues to work as Associate Professor in the same faculty and gives graduate, postgraduate, and doctorate lessons at the Department of Management and Organization. Furthermore, he serves as thesis advisor at postgraduate and doctorate level. His fields of specialization are human resource management and organizational behavior. He published numerous papers at national and international level. Ünsar is married and has a daughter. Prof. Unsar is member of International Group on Governance Fraud Ethics and Corporate Social Responsibility.

Chapter 1
Leadership

Leadership is one of the most important concepts of today. Considering that there is a managed group and managers both in societies and enterprises, it is observed that leadership, which is one of the most important elements of management, gains prominence. Like in every era, humans always needed and will need a leader when they come together. The method of managing humans in an effective and efficient manner depends on leadership process. Groups and societies feel secure thanks to their leaders and thus they become more successful. A leader enables communities to follow the right path confidently and safely. In addition, the efforts of the leader to establish and shape future are of great importance. This book firstly explains basic concepts about leadership and leadership theories and then communication and communication theories. Finally, it presents the study on this subject and the results of the study.

1.1 The Concept of Leadership

The concept of leadership has been analyzed, discussed and studied from the past to the present. A person, whom we call leader, is needed in any place where there are people or certain groups. It can be stated that a person whom we call leader appears in any place where there is a group of people. Considering that groups always need an orientation, leaders had always been and will always be present. On the other hand, it can be stated that every state and enterprise will create their own leaders when appropriate conditions are formed.

It involves orientating the group to a previously determined aim and to use the power of the humans in the groups at a certain direction in an effective and correct manner. This can only be achieved by the leaders who know the group and recognize the followers.

Analysis of the historical process from the past to the present reveals that certain people differed from others and managed to lead masses of people. When we analyze the historical process, we see political, military and social leaders who

S. Ünsar, *Leadership and Communication*, Contributions to Management Science, DOI 10.1007/978-3-319-05248-9_1, © Springer International Publishing Switzerland 2014

made their marks in history. The difference of leaders particularly arises in the process of influencing their followers.

These leaders became the leaders of the mentioned societies as they differed from other people in the society and they influenced other individuals due to their superior characteristics. We can show Mustafa Kemal ATATÜRK, the founder of Republic of Turkey, as an example of the mentioned leadership.

In addition, the fact that they showed different leadership behaviors at changing conditions or displayed the leadership behavior required by the present situation enabled them to appear as a leader.

Since understanding the concept of leadership involves a highly complicated and emotional process, number of studies on leadership gradually increases. A reason for this increase is that there is no clear definition for leadership; another reason is that there are available factors to improve and evaluate the leaders to make them more effective (Kesken and Ayyıldız 2008:730).

Today there is a need for leaders in this globalizing world in political, economic etc. fields at national and international level. It can be stated that each organization will create its own leader. In other words, a leader will appear in line with the conditions and needs of the organization.

There is a growing need for effective leaders who will influence and motivate the groups in organizations and enterprises and to enable them to progress in line with their given objectives. There are many definitions and statements about leadership. These definitions are sometimes similar or different. However, they were all made to define a leader in the best manner. Some of these definitions are explained below.

Leadership is the process of orientating or effecting behaviors and activities of other people by one person to fulfill predetermined objectives of a person or group under certain conditions. It can be stated that a certain objective will be achieved as a result of this process (Koçel 2005:583).

A leader is a member of a group who has the abilities of planning, organization, convincing and motivation (Eren 2007:432).

Leadership is the process of supporting and influencing people with a stirring and voluntary manner to fulfill predetermined objectives. It can be stated that leaders will make their followers to achieve their aims by stirring them up (Newstrom and Davis 2002:163).

Truman, one of the previous presidents of the United States, defined leadership as the person who has the ability to make his/her followers ready to perform behaviors that they don't want to do. On the other hand, Eisenhover defined leadership as the ability to decide on what to do and to make their followers be willing to do that (Budak and Budak 2004:380).

A leader is a person who has good ideas on which everyone accepts and agrees; who are followed by everyone and who has the power to realize an objective (Hogg and Vaughan 2007:346).

Leadership is the art of making the followers to do things that they don't want to do and to manage to make them to be satisfied with what they had done (Bender 2000:15).

People who have behaviors to enable job satisfaction and efficiency and the ability of intercultural interaction are called leaders. Thus, it can be stated that improving job satisfaction and efficiency of people working under one's command is an important characteristic of a leader (Uyargil et al. 2008:39).

Leadership can be defined as the process of orientating group activities based on identification and improvement of group objectives (Tengilimoğlu and Yiğit 2005:377).

Leadership is a dynamic process and a situation related to communication process, interpersonal behavior and motivation (Mullins 1996:246).

Leadership is a combination of ability and knowledge to gather a certain group of people in line with certain aims and to motivate them to achieve predetermined objectives (Eren 2003:525).

A leader is the person who can express that his/her instructions are a part of the conditions and situations; who can consider the situation as a whole and who can determine reciprocal interactions and dependencies within the complete in the best manner (Baransel 1993:268).

Leadership is teaching, rearing, appointing, transferring, stirring up, giving advice, coaching, protecting and observing (Karalar 2010:70).

A leader is the person, who integrates the efforts of people working in organizations to fulfill predetermined objectives; who applies them; enables those people to show all their skills and who orientates them to the vision in an effective manner (Barutçugil 2004:488).

Based on the definitions and expressions above, it can be stated that leadership is a power and process which is effective in motivating a certain group or society to act at a certain direction. In addition, it can be stated that the leaders should be aware of all their abilities that they will use to achieve their aims or the power that have and should use this power and ability on the followers. In addition, we can state that influencing, satisfying and leading followers are the common properties of leadership process.

The concept of leader gains various meanings according to the context it is used. For example, in military terms, a leader means the person who leads and commands. In biology, leadership is a behavior specific to animals which leads animal flock and regulates social relationships. Here, the leader has the abilities to move quickly and fast. On the other hand, in the field of management, a leader means the people who influence persons, groups and organizations and orientates them to a certain objective (Aykan 2004:215).

Can a person born to be a leader? Can any person be a leader? Majority of researchers agree with both. Thus, it can be stated that this question is constantly discussed. Effective leaders are not born to be leaders or they did not become leaders. They are born with certain leadership abilities and then improve these abilities. If it was impossible to improve leadership abilities, important companies would not spend millions of dollars to leadership trainings each year. On the other hand, some researchers and experts report that a person is not born to be a leader; that any person can certainly be a leader and that everyone has equal potential of management. Legendary football coach Vince Lombardi stated that no one is born to be a leader and that a person can be a leader by making effort and by hard work. In general terms, it can be stated that leadership is a mixture of certain intrinsic characteristics specific to a person and knowledge acquired through education or experience. In other words, leadership is a synthesis with an artistic and academic aspect (Lussier and Achua 2010:9).

Humans can improve themselves in terms of leadership by seeking and acquiring new experiences. Today, educators now pay more attention to arising needs and demands towards leader training schools. Leadership courses and institutes are gradually being included in the curricula of developing schools. Thus, it can be stated that leadership has an academic aspect which is thought later (Ambrose 1991:118).

There are various types of leaders in leadership process. Leadership types according to Max Weber are presented below (Özsalmanlı 2005:138):

- Charismatic Leader: a leader type prepared by economic, historical, traditional and cultural conditions; who has intrinsic and revolutionary characteristics.
- Legal Leader: a leader type whose management power and authority towards his/her followers is based on law.
- A leader type whose power is based on traditions.

1.2 The Difference Between a Leader and a Manager

Analysis of the concepts of leader and manager reveals that both concepts motivate and orientate a certain group. Both concepts dominate communities or groups consisting of a certain number of people. However, it cannot be stated that these concepts have the same meaning. In other words, the concepts of leader and manager do not have the same meaning. For example, in enterprises there are people who have manager role, but who lack leadership characteristics; and the people who have no manager role despite having leadership characteristics. In other words, a person has the title of manager, however lacks the characteristics of a leader; or a person has leadership characteristic but lacks the title of a manager (Koçel 2005:584).

Leaders make effort to influence people; however managers work to ensure the continuation of the structure and system. In other words, while the leaders make effort to influence people, managers make effort to protect the existing organizational structure. The managers protect, but cannot change the existing aspect; but the leaders have the power to influence their followers to a new direction. Thus, it can be stated that managers have a static structure while the leaders have dynamic structure (Maxwell 1999b:21).

Analysis power and high energy in practice play a determinative role in the success of leaders. Some leaders gain prominence in terms of planning and follow-up, however there is a matter in which a leader cannot lack: decision process. The ability of quick decision making in a timely manner and under difficult conditions when required and bravery is the most important characteristic that distinguishes a leader from a manager. It can be stated that real leaders are the people who can make decisions quickly and accurately and can immediately apply these decisions (Kozlu 2009:55).

In addition, a leader is the person who can predict the move a person will make and behaves accordingly. Although they might not anticipate this situation, at least they behave in favor of themselves. As a result, it can be stated that a leader should have a high prediction and intuition power (Friedman 2009:30).

Managers make effort to deal with a complicated situation; their methods and applications are mostly a reaction to the emergence of complex and huge organizations in the past century. However, leadership involves the efforts to mostly deal with change. As we previously stated, since leaders have a dynamic structure, they make effort to constantly improve and change the existing situation and conditions (Vural and Coşkun 2007:95–96).

While a manager is not necessarily accepted or behaviorally followed by the people in the group; a leader is the person who is followed by all of the members in the group. This difference depends on the acceptance of the members in the group rather than authority. In addition, while a manager is a person who only solves problems and makes decisions; a leader has the characteristics to address to the needs of his/her followers and to satisfy their emotions. As a result, it can be stated that a leader should constantly develop communication level with the followers. On the other hand, to influence people, a leader should be in constant communication with them (Erdoğan 1997:332).

Effective leaders are specialized in coordination of team work, avoiding from conflict that damages the organization, evaluating different perspectives and achieving consensus. This specialization gives the leader the opportunity to develop positive relationships in achieving his/her aims. It can be stated that leaders should manage existing conflicts by establishing coordination between their followers like a conductor (Acar 2002:56)

While some people are leaders due to their formal positions in an organization, others are regarded as leaders as group members (their followers) respect them. These two types are two common types of leadership which are termed as "on duty leadership" and "sudden emerging leadership" (Northouse 2010:5).

Sam Walton, the founder of Walmart, spent his time wandering in stores and taking notes rather than sitting in president room and analyzing profit-loss tables. As a result, he detected the problems in situ and listened to suggestions. Like the proverb "Wandering fox is better than sitting lion" denotes, leaders should be involved in working field and identify existing problems in situ instead of sitting in their offices and waiting for problems. Managers don't use or don't want to use their imagination much; however, a leader derives all his/her power from imagination (Tekin 2008:39).

Basic differences between a leader and a manager are presented in Table 1.1.

Table 1.1 Basic differences between a leader and manager (Karalar 2010:109)

Leader	Manager
Enjoys change	Receives orders
Focuses on future, long-term and further	Focuses on the present time, short-term and lower line
Performs the correct work	Performs the works correctly
Gives importance to both emotion and cause	Gives more importance to cause than emotions
Takes risks	Involves the risks

1.3 The Role and Importance of a Leader

Leadership creates a personnel philosophy which knows what to do and where to go and which is aware of what one is doing. Organizations which lack a leader cannot determine a mission, vision and goal for the future. The prerequisite of being living organizations of future is to have a strong leader with a vision. If an enterprise lacks a leader, organizations turn out to be only a heap of human and machine. It was observed, heard or read that regardless of their positions, majority of leaders managed to achieve superior success through plans or inspections with insufficient or scarce possibilities. Selection of correct people, motivation techniques used in orientating these people to tasks, evaluation process and abilities in development are the factors that make leaders successful and important. Thus, it can be stated that a leader should also be a good skill hunter (Bilgin et al. 2004:7).

Leadership is applied through character. Character is a factor that the followers take as a model, mimic and try to look like. It is impossible to deceive the followers in terms of character. The followers can understand whether their leaders are honest or not within a couple of weeks. They can forgive the leader for many things. They can ignore inadequate self-confidence, lack of manners or knowledge; however they never forgive dishonesty. In addition, they also don't forgive the upper management who chose that leader. It is understood that humans can forgive everything except unethical behaviors of their leaders (Maciariello 2005:3).

The leaders managing organizations or countries have many duties such as selection of human resources, communication, change, vision formation, team building, structuring organization, adoption and establishment of core values (Akdemir 2008:66).

Many researchers defined four specific factors about the nature of researcher leadership. The first one: leadership is related with the change of thoughts and ideas. The second one: leadership requires impressing others. The third one: leadership appears within the context of group in addition to bilateral relationships. The fourth one: leadership requires fulfilling the aims and being successful (Kan and Parry 2004:468).

Principle duties of a leader can be listed as follows: determining the aims of organization, ensuring atmosphere and structure to the organization to achieve these aims, ensuring the organization to survive according to determined objectives and solving the conflicts between the followers (Atar and Özbek 2009:51).

In the logo of an apparel brand, a girl and a boy sit by leaning on their backs. I believe that leaders should never turn their backs to their subordinates like the figures do in this logo. If they do so, they and their companies can lose after a certain time. This indicates that communication is a constant and face-to-face process. A good leader should establish good one-to-one communication with their subordinates and should achieve to continue this in a successful manner.

An effective leader has the power to take the people to the places where they cannot go on their own. An effective leader can be considered as a person who can foresee the future; use his/her power appropriately; who is honest, reliable; can take lessons from mistakes; who is aware of his/her power; supports changes; egalitarian; supportive; inspiring; who expresses his/her views clearly; who listens to other people well and makes objective assessments; who supports his/her group; respects other people's opinions and has effective communication and management skills (Yiğit 2002:17).

The factor that vitalizes the enterprises and makes them dynamic is the leaders they have. Since the leaders have a critical perspective towards the existing situation, they constantly reject the existing structure. They constantly seek progress and innovation. They inspire and guide their followers about what they can do using their personal visions and abilities (Şimşek et al. 2008:242).

A shoe brand has an advertorial slogan of "just want it". In fact, this slogan contains a great motivation. If a person wants something very much and can canalize all his/her strength to that point, he/she can achieve it. Like the saying "No wind can help the ship without a route" denotes, leaders should have an objective or aim to fulfill. Leaders with an objective can succeed by making their subordinates adopt them and by providing necessary equipment. In other words, leaders should first themselves believe that they will achieve the aim, and then should make their subordinates believe it. Thus, they can achieve the aim by creating synergy.

The role of the leaders is commonly visible in huge organizations in a striking and considerable manner. Like in the case of Jack Welch, the CEO of General Electric, who brilliantly carried General Electric firm to the twenty-first century which could be considered as a sleeping giant in 1980s. Jack Welch began to run General Electric, which was not in a good situation and created considerable wind of change in the enterprise (Davis and Newstrom 2002:163).

A tire firm as an advertorial slogan of "uncontrolled power is not the power". A good leader is strong and can use this power on his/her subordinates in a controlled manner. What is important is not to have the power, but to use it in an effective and controlled manner to achieve the aims. Similar to the water retained in a dam and used for desired aims (electric production, agricultural irrigation), power can be regarded in the same manner. Like uncontrolled flood water destroys everything around, uncontrolled power can similarly damage the environment. Therefore, it can be stated that the leaders should use their power in a controlled manner to contribute to the aims of the group. On the other hand, in addition to using the existing power, the leaders should be knowledgeable about the potential of their power.

Alfred Sloan, legendary leader of General Motors, gave importance to the views and opinions of his followers about a certain matter in the company. Sloan included his followers in different committees and involved these groups in discussions which would end with compromise. As a result, a good leader is the person who gives importance to the views and opinions of his/her followers and creates free environment where they can express these views and opinions comfortably and freely (Freeman 2008:36).

According to Akın Öngör, one of the previous general managers of Garanti Bank, a leader is not only a person who remains at the top position and occupies a position. He believes that the person who is called as a leader, should be the leader of what his/her work no matter what work he/she performs instead of simply implementing the orders of his/her managers and to wait for instructions. In other words, no matter what they do, the managers should adopt the areas they work and should perform the best one. If everyone in a street cleans in front of his/her house, the whole street becomes clean. Similarly, each manager in the company should perform his/her duty in the best manner (Öngör 2010:120).

Leadership is the final movement that carries the organization, the people in that organization and all potential to success. The leaders use their ability, creativity and vision for the product and services which are the essence of the work. In other words, the leaders put their souls in what they do. The managers apply their personal intelligence to the work process; they feel excitement about managing the company. The organizations which want to progress should invest in leaders (Ünsar 2007:3).

While some leaders seclude themselves using all of their possessions to develop themselves and receive 360° feedback or guidance from their colleagues, some leaders get engaged in art or music (Gerson 2006:80).

A good leader should know his/her subordinates he/she leads very well. Furthermore, he/she should know what their subordinates like, get angry for or what motivates them; he/she even should know their shoe and apparel size. In this way, as the leader gets to know them better, he/she will reach information that will motivate them. I have a simple formula about this issue: "You get to know= If you listen". If we listen to the people, we learn their unknown strong aspects; we can create environments that enable them to express their views and opinions and thus we have the opportunity to know our subordinates better. As a person listens to the other, he/she gets to know them better; as he/she gets to know them better, he/she provides a more effective and efficient management environment and opportunity. In this manner, a leader gives his/her subordinates, who saw that they were taken into account by their leaders and increased self-confidence, the opportunity to develop original ideas, opinions and suggestions.

Much of previous research found that people were happier and more productive in groups lead by good leaders while hopelessness and alienation increased in groups lead by bad leaders. As a result, it can be stated that a leader has a significant psychological role in the success of his/her followers and that a good leader makes his/her followers happy while a bad leader makes them unhappy (Baltaş 2010:72).

Napoleon Bonaparte is known as a dealer in hope. He considered hope as the most important thing a person has. If a leader can give hope to his/her followers as a present, he/she can attract them like a magnet and can raise respect. It can be stated that giving or distributing hope provides motivation on employees (Maxwell 1999a:16).

An effective and efficient leadership depends on contribution of the leader to the fulfillment of group aims and members' appreciation that needs of the group are satisfied. On the other hand, internal dynamics of the organization such as changing environmental conditions, planning deficiencies, status and roles, communication system, atmosphere of the organization and participation to decisions can be listed as the principle reasons for the need for a leader in the organization. In other words, it can be stated that certain needs increase the need to a leader (Özsalmanlı 2005:138).

1.4 Leadership Theories

Leadership maintains its popularity as the commonly handled and studies concept in many countries around the world. The questions as to what leadership is, how it is formed and whether it is congenital or acquired and developed later have long drew the attention of many researchers.

Previous studies developed numerous theories about leadership. It can be stated there is a continuing research on leadership. These theories answer many questions about leadership. Leadership theories can be analyzed under four groups:

A) Traits Theory
B) Behavioral Theories
C) Situational (Conditional) Theories
D) Modern Leadership Theories

Leadership theories are explained below.

1.4.1 Traits Theory

In this theory, the traits the leaders have are considered to be the most important factors affecting the process. Emergence of a person in the group as the leader and leading the group by impressing the group are based on the traits of the leader. Traits theory assumes that the leader has different traits than other people in the group (Ertürk 2009a:152).

Congenital traits or certain skills and characteristics the people have will influence their leadership behavior in the future. The ability to express oneself well, having superior intelligence and patience can be listed as the characteristics that contribute to leadership. In fact, there are studies which show that certain traits and abilities have a vital importance for leadership (Drake and Smith 1990:213).

This theory suggests that the majority of the traits the leaders have are congenital and that they cannot be acquired later. Based on the studies on leadership traits, the traits a leader should have can be analyzed in four categories which are emotional, physical, social and intellectual traits (Budak and Budak 2010a:79–80).

Emotional Traits: Sense of confidence, ambition, controlling oneself, perception, a strong sense of achievement.

Physical Traits: Being attractive, gender, height, age, eloquence.

Social Traits: Friendship, extraverted personality structure, establishing good communication with others.

Intellectual Traits: Initiative, vision, persuasion, intelligence, determinism, attention, ability.

1.4.2   Behavioural Theories

Traits approach explains the traits a leader should have. However, it can be stated that it is not always possible to make a connection between the traits of the leaders and the performance they show and that the leaders who are successful in their fields do not always have the same traits. For these reasons, researchers began to investigate visible leadership actions and behaviors. They analyzed and attempted to estimate the difference between successful and less successful leaders in terms of their behavioral traits. Scientific studies were carried out at Michigan and Ohio State Universities to determine behavioral aspect of leadership (Özkalp and Kırel 2004:148). These studies are explained below.

1.4.2.1   Ohio State University Leadership Studies

The studies which started in 1945 in Ohio State University continued until early 1950s. A total of 1,800 dimensions were produced about leadership roles. These dimensions were then reduced to 150. A "Leader behavior identification questionnaire" was developed. The study carried out at the university aimed to investigate the behaviors of leaders in groups in different organizations (Baysal and Tekarslan 1998:206).

The researchers determined two principle dimensions about leader behaviors which were "initiating structure" and "consideration". Providing the subordinates with the list of the tasks they will perform, planning and determining aims, deciding on what kinds of tasks will be performed and oppressing the subordinates about the tasks they will perform can be the examples of initiating structure. On the other hand, consideration is a dimension which expresses respect, trust and positive relationships and interactions between the leader and his/her followers. If a leader has a high level of consideration, he gives importance to the well-being, ideas and emotions of his/her followers (Güney et al 2007:363).

In other words, consideration dimension means establishing friendship with the followers and giving them due importance by the leader (Ertürk 2009b:156).

These two dimensions allow to identify the style of the individual, to define the leader as he/she is perceived by the followers in the organization and to measure leadership behaviors (Durukan et al. 2006:5).

It can be stated that considering each of the two behavioral dimensions identified in Ohio State University studies as independent variables and regarding the these variables will produce leader behaviors at equal number with different combinations of these variables made this study different from Michigan University studies (Ergeneli 2006:219).

1.4.2.2 Michigan University Leadership Studies

At the end of 1940s, a study was carried out at Michigan University under the supervision of Rensis Likert to determine the factors that cause job satisfaction and productivity of group members (Koçel 2010:579).

The study determined two principle leadership behaviors which were "employee-centered" and "task-centered" behaviors (Bakan 2008:16).

A leader who shows employee-centered behavior has a positive attitude towards delegation of authority; increases job satisfaction of group members, pays attention to improving working conditions and values personal development of employees. On the other hand, a leader who shows task-oriented behavior inspects whether group members work according to previously determined rules and standards and mostly uses his/her formal power based on the position he/he holds (Çetin and Beceren 2007:127).

The study conducted at Michigan University concluded that employee-oriented leadership behavior was more effective than task-oriented behavior. In this study, employee-orientated leaders were associated with high level of efficiency and job satisfaction while task-oriented leaders were associated with low level of personnel satisfaction (Budak and Budak 2010a:83)

1.4.2.3 Douglas Mc Gregor's Theory X and Theory Y

Douglas McGregor claims that the behaviors of managers working in organizations vary according to their way of perceiving their subordinates. He developed Theory X and Theory Y about the natural structure of humans (Şahin 2004:532).

Principle assumptions of Theory X are listed below: (Mucuk 2008:167–168):

– An average person does not like working and is lazy; he/she avoids work whenever possible.

- People must be coerced, controlled or threatened with punishment in order to get them work and make effort.
- Since an average person has limited ambition to promotion, they don't want responsibility; prefer to be directed and seek security.

Principle assumptions of Theory X are listed below: (Kaynak 1990:38–39).

- Spending mental and physical strength in working environment is as natural as rest and play.
- People exercise self-inspection and self-direction while performing their tasks.
- Giving an employee a task again due to his/her achievement will be a sort of reward for him/her.
- Under certain conditions, people learn to take and seek responsibility.
- The society has high imagination and creativity required to solve organizational problems.

Analysis of Theory Y of McGregor reveals that trust factor is of great importance. Premises of theory Y contain statements that ensure trust to the employee in terms of business relations within the organization (Asunakutlu 2001:12). A general analysis of Theories of X and Y shows that a leader who adopts Theory of X will have to constantly control, coerce, threaten and punish their employees to achieve a high employee success. On the other hand, a leader who adopts Theory of Y will show a supportive and participative behavior towards their employees. In other words, it can be stated that the leaders who adopt theory of X will show authoritative behaviors while the leaders who adopt theory of Y will show democratic leadership behaviors (Davis 1984:13–14).

1.4.2.4   The Blake Mouton Managerial Grid

As indicated in Fig. 1.1, this model involves two dimensions. The first one is concerned with people in manager behaviors; the second one is concerned with production in manager behaviors. A total of five different managerial behavior types were determined with different combinations of these two dimensions (Eren 2007:36). Concern for people expresses a perspective in all matters such as trust to all workers in the organization, establishing good communication and relationship, forming an equal wage structure and forming good working conditions while achieving organizational objectives. On the other hand, concern for production expresses a perspective of the managers in matters such as developing new products, improving processes, determining politics and attempts to increase sales (Aksel 2008:41).

In managerial grid model, Black and Mouton defined five leadership styles which are Impoverished Leadership, Country Club Leadership, Middle-of-the-Road Leadership, Produce or Perish Leadership and Team Leadership. Impoverished Leadership lacks both leadership dimensions. Country Club Leadership has a high concern for people dimension. In middle-of-the-road Leadership,

Fig. 1.1 Black and Mouton
Managerial grid (Newstrom
and Davis 2002:170)

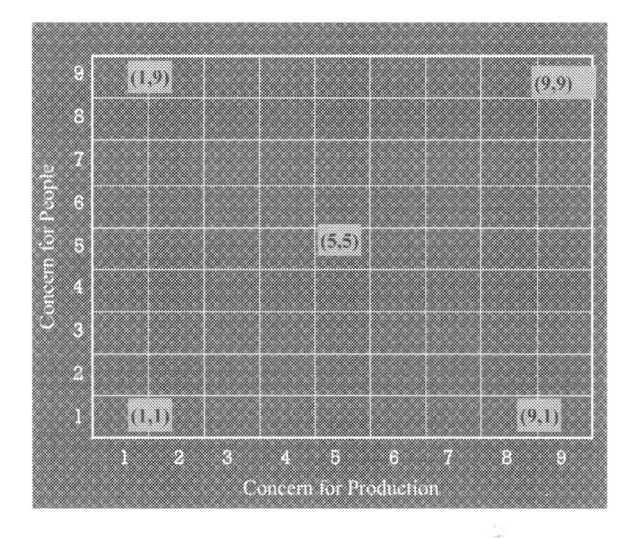

both dimensions are at a moderate level. In Produce or Perish leadership, concern
for production is high. In team leadership, both dimensions are at a high level
(Budak and Budak 2004:401–402).

1.4.2.5   System 4 Approach of Rensis Likert

In this model, which was developed by Rensis Likert based on Michigan University
studies, leader behaviors were categories in four systems (Baysal and Tekarslan
1998:212). These systems are explained below.

In system 1, the manager rarely gives his/her subordinates the opportunity to
participate in decision-making process and does not trust them. In system 2, the
manager trusts his/her subordinates and his trust is in the form of a trust a master
shows to his/her servants. In system 3, the manager shows an important however
uncompleted trust towards his/her subordinates. Finally, in system 4, the management completely trusts to subordinates. Decision-making is distributed to the
general of the organization in a coordinated manner (Eren 1993:30–31)

1.4.3   Situational (Conditional) Theories

Leadership theories explained above does not take into account the environment, in
other words, the conditions. Traits theory only explains the traits leaders should
have while behavioral theories concentrate on whether a leader is concentrated on
the aims of the group or on their followers. Need to leadership appears in situations
to achieve vital goals or to solve unbearable problems. In other words, problematic
situations produce the leader (Başaran 2004:90).

Researchers attempt to find the type of leadership behavior that will be effective in certain conditions. In parallel to changing conditions, the leaders should determine and implement the optimum leadership type like the masters that use different tools from their tool box to solve a problem (Arslan 2009:5).

In other words, situational approach suggests that different conditions should show different leadership styles. Theories on situational approach are explained below (Koçel 2010:584).

1.4.3.1 Fiedler's Contingency Theory

Studies on the contingency in leadership started for the first time by Fred Fiedler, who developed the least preferred co-worker scale to measure leadership behaviors. According to this model, there are three important situational variables that affect the role and strength of the leader and which determine the most suitable leadership situation (Mullins 1996:265). These variables are explained below.

Leader-Member relations: at this stage, the leader is loved by group members and voluntarily followed.

Task structure: at this stage, tasks for the group are clearly defined and standard methods to be followed and detailed instructions for the task are identified.

Position power: power of the leader results from his/her power within the organization. At this stage, the leader influences the followers using reward, punishment, promotion and downgrading (Mullins 1996:266).

According to Fiedler, combination of all three situational variables explained above determines whether low LPC or high LPC leadership style is appropriate. In other words, when situational variables are negative, mostly task-oriented low leadership is shown. On the other hand, when situational leadership variables are positive, employee-oriented high LPC leadership behavior is shown. If the mentioned variables are at moderate level, employee-oriented high LPC leadership behavior is appropriate (Dessler 1998:346).

In general terms, this theory divides leaders into two categories which are task-oriented or relationship-oriented. Task-oriented leaders can be shown as an example to authoritative leader; while relationship-oriented leaders can be shown as an example to participative and democratic leader (Özkalp and Sabuncuoğlu 1990:145)

In a study carried out on infantry soldiers, it was observed that increased commanding and training experience of team leader shifted from relationship-oriented relationship to task-oriented relationship. In other words, it was observed that at first task-oriented leadership style was less effective, however this style became more effective after the leader gained experience and increased control on the situation (Taylor et al. 2010:339).

In general terms, this model investigates which leadership style should be applied under certain conditions. As a result, it can be stated that effectiveness of leadership styles depends on showing the most appropriate leadership behavior under the most important conditions (Koçel 2010:588).

1.4.3.2 The Hersey and Blanchard Situational Leadership Theory

According to this model, success of leaders depends on the maturity levels of followers. The concept of maturity means how motivated the followers are to perform their tasks, how much experience they gained, how sufficient they are and how enthusiastic they are to take responsibility. Maturity involves two situations. Psychological maturity and task maturity. Psychological maturity expresses the enthusiasm and willingness of the person to perform the task while task maturity involves the extent the individual has knowledge, skills and ability required to perform his/her task (Ergeneli 2006:228).

Leadership behaviors proposed according to development levels and development level of the employee are presented in Table 1.2. On the other hand, The Hersey and Blanchard Situational Leadership Theory is presented in Fig. 1.2.

1.4.3.3 Path-Goal Theory

This model was developed by Martin Evans and Robert House. The researchers reported that the leader has two important functions in the organization (Kırel et al. 2004:158).

The researchers stated that they realized two important functions which are determining organizational goals and ensuring that determined aims are achieved by supporting their employees in line with desired behaviors and by explaining them which aims will be rewarded (Özkalp and Kırel 2004:152).

House defined four types of leadership behaviors: directive leader, supportive leader, participative leader and achievement oriented leader (Mullins 1996:269–270).

Although path-goal approach explains leadership with different variables, it is based on contingency. It was explained that considering the existing situations, effectiveness of leader requires choosing one of task-oriented or employee-oriented behaviors (Tekarslan et al. 2000:148).

According to a general evaluation of the approach, the contributions of this approach to leadership can be listed as follows: motivating the employees and increasing efficiency, making the tasks clear and precise and eliminating monotonousness by focusing on socio-psychological needs of employees (Eren 2007:456–457).

1.4.3.4 Three Dimensional Leadership Model

This approach, which was developed by William Reddin, mainly gives importance to what the leader realizes as an outcome, in other words, as an output; rather than what he/she performs as input. A leader might make 100 % effort as input; however he/she might have zero effectiveness as output. For example, a copying machine

Table 1.2 Leadership styles recommended according to development level of the employee
(Newstrom and Davis 2002:173)

Development level of the employee	Behavioral style of leader
Low competence; low willingness	Telling (instructing; low support)
Low competence; high willingness	Selling/Coaching (instructing; supporting)
High competence; low willingness	participating/supporting (supporting; low directing)
High competence; high willingness	Delegating; (low directing; low support)
Takes risks	Includes risks

Fig. 1.2 Hersey and
Blanchard situational
leadership model (Baysal
and Tekarslan 1998:236)

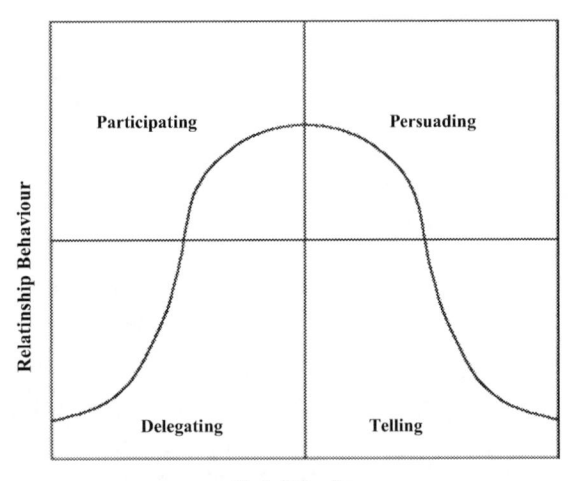

Task Behaviour

marketer can visit a lot of customers but might not realize the desired sale (Baysal
and Tekarslan 1998:231).

Reddin added "the concept of effectiveness" to managerial grid and Ohio State
University studies and reported that leadership showed variations on three basic
dimensions. Therefore, the theory of Reddin is known as 3-D Model, which stands
for "Three Dimensional" theory (Ömürgönülşen and Sevim 2005:93).

Reddin's theory is based on the concept of "managerial effectiveness". Reddin
suggested that principle aim of management was effectiveness and defined "managerial effectiveness" as the degree of fulfilling necessary things required by the
position of a leader (Gönülşen and Sevim 2005:92).

Reddin defined five situational variables such as organizational culture, chief
supervisor, the way the task is performed, co-workers and subordinates for the
effectiveness of managers. The researcher stated that if the managers analyze and
understand these variables, their and their employees' performance will be
improved (Safferstone 2007:4).

1.4.4 Modern Leadership Theroies

Moderrn leadership theories were analyzed in this Section.

1.4.4.1 Transactional Leadership

This is a leadership style in which the acts of rewarding according to performance, identification of the ones which deviate from rules and processes and display of excellent behaviors gain prominence. Bureaucratic authority and organizational legality form the basis of leadership (Özmen and Sönmez 2007:190).

Transactional leaders adopt the system of doing work or making other people do work by making their continuing activities more effective and developed. The leaders use their authority to give a material reward and status to make their employees make more effort. They don't pay attention to innovative or creative aspects of their employees. Transactional leaders have some degree of traditional structure and try to continue beneficial traditions of the past and to convey them to next generations (Tutar et al. 2009:388).

A transactional leader fulfills the wishes of employees and expects their support. On the other hand, while this leadership style is based on bureaucratic and legal power in the organization, it also gives importance to completion of task and organizational reward. A transactional leader keeps the expectations and needs of the employees at a high level and attaches a particular importance to moral values (Altun 2003:11).

These types of leaders use means of reward and punishment to establish authority on their followers (Uzun 2005:5).

Transactional leaders consider leader-follower interaction as a sort of "exchange" and make effort to implement management techniques duly and efficiently (Bakan 2008:17).

1.4.4.2 Transformational Leadership

Transformational leaders are considered as the ones who can influence the emotions and opinions of their followers and have strong and positive emotions (Vural 1997:21).

These types of leaders teach their employees how to think creatively on the existing problems by forming the feeling of trust and aim (Taylo et al. 2010:339).

Transformational leadership consists of four behavior dimensions. In "Idealized Influence" dimension, the leader introduces the followers the mission and vision and becomes the role model. "Inspirational Motivation" dimension is described as team spirit, shared vision and inspiration for the group to achieve their goals. "Intellectual Stimulation" dimension expresses the process of stimulating creativity, innovation and problem solving characteristics on the followers. Finally, in

"Individual Consideration" dimension the leaders pay attention to each followers' needs and creates a supportive environment for them (Simola et al. 2010:180).

Transformational leadership is closely related with charismatic leadership and spiritual leadership. Today this leadership style draws more attention since it plays an important role in realizing a successful and striking change in organizations. Lee Laccocca is often shown as an example to this leadership style since he successfully realized a fundamental change in Chrysler Company (Certo 2003:342).

Transformational leadership is a leadership style which gives the followers a vision where contributing to this vision gives additional missions to the followers. Transformational leadership makes changes in organizational culture and makes the followers believe that that can do much more than their existing performance or potentials by providing cultural change. In other words, transformational leadership, transformational leadership inspires the followers to perform more than what was desired at the beginning (Bolat and Seymen 2003:64).

Transformational leaders undertake the role of a teacher to develop their followers and to make them reach their full potential and take responsibility by making effort to facilitate the works (Barut et al. 2010:133).

These types of leaders try to make their followers show a higher performance than what is expected from them by revealing their existing skills and abilities, increasing their self-esteem and by motivating them (Eren 2007:460–461).

Previous studies emphasized the importance of transformational leadership which involves inspiration, vision and long-term planning in periods of change when shaping the future gains prominence (Doğanalp 2009:135).

Basic characteristics of transformational leadership include leading desired efforts of change in an organization and making the followers have a vision. In this leadership style, the leader arranges the behaviors and actions to change the structure of the organization on his/her own (Şahin and Gül 2011:241–242).

Transformational leaders offer opportunities in developing the image of the organization, recruitment, promotion, diversification of management, team work, training and improvement issues. In addition, strategic planning of organization and design of works and organizational structure can be included in these opportunities (Bass 1998:81)

In a study carried out on Chinese organizations, it was found that particularly employee-oriented transformational leadership behavior had a stronger impact on task performance, organizational citizenship behavior and job satisfaction than task-centered transformational leadership behavior (Wang et al. 2011:94).

Transformational leaders show due attention to individual needs of their followers and often assign them basic tasks in line with their needs and abilities (Whittington 2004:595).

In a previous study it was reported that transformational leadership behavior was the most effective and efficient element in formation of leadership (Osborn and Marion 2000:193). In another study, it was verified that transformational leaders had positive impacts on development and performance of their followers (Daft 2008:508).

Since global business circles will be more competitive in the future, managers will constantly make a significant change in their organizations. For this reason, it can be stated that transformational leadership will gradually gain more importance in the literature (Certo 2003:342).

1.4.4.3 Charismatic Leadership

Charisma is a Greek word which means gift and is used for people having exceptional power and divinely traits and powers (Güney et al. 2007:374). The important thing here is attribution of such characteristics to the leader rather than leader's actually having these features (Kongar 1983:130).

Charisma is a characteristic that enables the followers to follow the leader since they trust them. It can be defined as the ability to inspire the followers (Whitney 2007:19).

Charisma is trait which makes the leader attractive, reliable and obeyed for the followers. This trait can be associated with the attraction of iron by magnet (Özalp and Öcal 2000:215).

This leadership is based on the principle of attributing extraordinary and heroic characteristics to the leader by the followers due to behaviors shown by him/her. Superior emotional power the leader has deeply influences the followers and thus the leader becomes glorious in the eyes of the followers (Çakar and Arbak 2003:84).

Charismatic leaders are influential leaders who motivate their followers and create trust on them to encourage them to reach superior performance. These leaders make effort to listen to the problems and feelings of their followers and to help them to achieve their own goals. The followers feel positive emotions towards this leader and perform their tasks with a great enthusiasm. A good leader is expected to have superior listening and motivating traits (Aykan,2004:215–216).

Charismatic leaders are the ones who make a change. They form a strong vision and establish a connection between the leader and the followers to change the thinking systems and behaviors of their followers. If a leader is a reliable leader and can express the rules of management, change will be quite easy. On the other hand, charismatic traits and behaviors of the leader provide identification with the leader and the followers. As a result, the leader and the followers meet at a common ground (Rowold and Heinitz 2007:122).

Charismatic leaders are the people with superior qualities recognized and trusted by the society, who generally appear during the times of distress in the group or in the society. These leaders are believed to have heavenly attributes. There is a similarity between the hopes and expectations of the society and the leader. On the other hand, they are regarded as a savior of the society or the group since these leaders bring a new perspective and impetus to the society (Taşdemir 2009:160).

Charismatic leaders are the great actors of leadership arena who persuade their followers and reflect self-confidence. They offer extraordinary solutions to extraordinary situations or problems. Since they don't experience a conflict between their impressions and emotions, they show determinism for events. In other words, these types of leaders can influence their followers with their courage, vision, self-confidence, values, speaking and persuasion abilities. In other words, leaders can influence the society with their superior qualities (Oktay and Gül 2003:405).

In addition to trusting and respecting the leader, the followers consider the leader as a hero. Charismatic leaders expect their followers to be boundlessly loyal to them (Yavuz 2009:53).

The qualities of charismatic leaders are listed below (Lussier and Achua 2010:341):

(a) visionary
(b) verbal skills
(c) self-confidence and moral conviction
(d) inspires trust
(e) high risk orientation
(f) high energy action orientation
(g) relational power based
(h) minimum internal conflict
(i) empowers others
(j) self-promoting

1.4.4.4 Autocratic Leadership

In autocratic leadership, decision-making authority is only held by the leader. The advantages of this leadership style can include the freedom of behaving independently and opportunity of taking faster and more effective decisions to autocratic leader. on the other hand, the disadvantages of this style include leader's excessively egoistic behavior and reducing motivation, job satisfaction and creativity skills of the followers by not giving them right to speak (Bakan and Büyükbeşe 2010:75).

Autocratic leaders determine the policy on their own without ever discussing with their followers or expecting their oppositions and impose them to their employees. These leaders determine reward and punishment on their own and practice as they like. It can be stated that autocratic leadership is suitable if the followers lack enough maturity (İnce 2006:19).

If autocratic leaders fail to change their strategic preferences and values despite strengthening their positions, they are likely to encounter resistance from their followers and to experience conflict. Authoritative leaders have absolute power; they have the right to ask for loyalty from their followers gratuitously. However, the followers are reluctant to obey and feel committed (Köksal 2011:106–107).

Autocratic leaders don't allow their followers to participate in management process. These leaders criticize mistakes, give instructions to influence and motivate their followers (Şahin et al. 2004:659).

1.4.4.5 Visionary Leadership

Visionary leaders are prescient people who can bring new horizons to the organizations. Visionary leaders inspire their followers in organizations to actively use their abilities and to perform good things. Future-oriented behaviors are important for visionary leadership (Aksu 2009:2439).

A visionary leader can successfully spread the vision he/she developed for the future to all departments of the organization. He/she can see the future from a different and new perspective and can make analysis and synthesis. This leader can influence his/her followers both with his/her power and thoughts (Durukan 2006:281–282).

Qualities of visionary leaders include strategic thinking, reasoning, honesty and intuition, self-development, multi-faceted and different perception of things, constant tendency to learning, good communication, innovation, good time management, considering change as an opportunity to learn (Bulut and Uygun 2010:34).

Visionary leaders enable their followers to make predictions about and accurate perception of potential future situations (Yılmaz and Karahan 2010:146).

Visionary leaders contribute to better understanding of long-term tasks by the followers and help to make continuing routine tasks meaningful. They develop a clear vision by combining the goals of the followers and organization (Avcı and Topaloğlu 2009:10).

Creative attributes of visionary leadership can be divided into four categories: creating respected and authorizing relationships; basic spiritual values, an open, inspiring vision and a source of innovation and courage in practice.

1.4.4.6 Democratic Leadership

In this leadership style, the leader does not behave only according to his/her own skills and knowledge; but also consults his/her followers and take their opinions and knowledge into account. As the leader fully trusts the followers in all matters, he/she motivates them to take part in decision-making, planning and organization activities. Democratic leadership can create job satisfaction and increased morale by laying the basis for communication and assistance and creating positive communication between the leader and the followers (Yörük et al. 2011:105).

Instead of centralizing responsibilities, a democratic leader shares them among the followers and thus enables each follower to take part in responsibility. He/she tries to solve the problems among the followers and to take objective measures instead of being a party. He/she tries to prevent formation of groups including followers with special privileges (Çeyiz 2007:25).

Principle activities and character of a democratic leader is to inform the followers, to increase their knowledge level, to behave in a friendly manner and to encourage them to participate. On the other hand, democratic leadership is related to increase efficiency, satisfaction, commitment and responsibility of followers (Choi 2007:245–247).

Democratic leaders are particularly effective when coordination and cooperation is necessary between the groups. These types of leaders show the following behaviors (Marquis and Huston 2009:38):

- Using economic and personal reward to motivate the followers,
- Including the followers in decision-making process,
- making constructive criticism,
- preferring "me and you" instead of emphasizing "we",
- reduced control in achieving continuity,
- leading the followers through guidance and suggestions.

In a study which analyzed the effects of leadership on group and determined leadership styles, it was reported that democratic leaders instill their followers with courage, give guiding advice and made cooperation with the followers (Baransel 1993:274).

1.4.4.7 Ethical Leadership

Basic duties of ethical leaders is to increase awareness about ethical problem and situations, to determine what is ethically correct and incorrect and to support their followers in analyzing and interpreting existing values (Arslantaş and Dursun 2008:112).

A leader should show ethical behaviors to influence his/her followers. Since the leaders who behave unethically cannot influence their followers, they will fail to make them adopt their visions. In that case, the followers cannot know what leader's mission will offer to the society, organization and to them and finally they will feel suspicion (Bolat and Seymen 2003:73).

The leaders of a plane company in the USA restored trust among their customers, employees and the public by using open communication following a series of ethical scandals they experienced in recent years (Daft 2008:260).

On the other hand, perception of ethical traits of a leader such as integrity and honesty will reinforce trust towards the leader and increase commitment (Özdaşlı and Yücel 2010:70).

1.4.4.8 Creative Leadership

Creative leaders contribute to supporting creativity instead of restricting it; thus they lay the basis of forming organizational climate and influence creativity of their followers. Creativity develops in organizations with flexibility and dynamism. To enhance creativity, leaders should first have an accurate perception of creative process, create organizational climate where creativity can easily appear and to reward creative behaviors (Yılmaz and Karahan 2010:147).

Leader's creative potential might accelerate motivation and group dynamism. These types of leaders can make phenomena abstract; they don't feel alarmed towards vagueness and are very practical. Rather than personal success, they give importance to the success of the group and show a close interest to the followers in the group. While trying to be a model for their followers with their attitudes and behaviors, they make attempt to make research and innovation (Yeloğlu 2007:139).

Changing century is the era of creative leaders. Turning organizations into flexible and sensitive structure as a result of changing identities, social pressure and needs of organizations, requires creative leaders. Creative leaders blend technological process and their followers into new organizations holding new values (Öztürk 2008:113–114).

Presence of inspiring creative leaders is an important factor to develop an effective information strategy for the enterprises. These leaders inspire and motivate their followers and create information required for the organization (Doğan and Kılıç 2009:105).

Some organizations are more sensitive to change than others. If an organization resists to change, this is probably because the leader accepts and doesn't reject existing paradigms. On the other hand, if an organization is in a process of change, it is probably because the leader either rejects the existing paradigms or makes a synthesis (Sternberg et al. 2003:471).

1.4.4.9 Educational Leadership

Educational leadership is generally defined as a combination of various tasks such as monitoring the existing class teaching, development of human resource and developing programs for the subject. Five principle tasks of educational leadership include making direct contribution to program development, group development, human resources development, educators and effectiveness research (Saygınar 2007:70).

1.4.4.10 Knowledge Leadership

Knowledge leadership is a process which creates a suitable working environment to derive knowledge and serves as a bridge between the leader and manager roles using management information systems. These types of leaders are needed in all fields of enterprises. Knowledge leaders form and use knowledge necessary to develop their effectiveness and that of the enterprises (Karahan 2009:64).

Information society has a growing need for sophisticated leaders with intellectual awareness, knowledge and skills, global thinking and strong thinking. In this era, since knowledge gained strategic value, organization structures are redesigned to be human-oriented and knowledge based management systems; knowledge leaders try to lead their followers to use their mental power for effective production (Tikici 2005:233).

1.4.4.11   Servant Leadership

Servant leadership is based on the process of establishing one-to-one communication with the followers to identify their individual abilities, need, desires, goals and potential at the optimum level. After determining the characters and interests of the followers, the leader provides necessary help required by each to achieve their goals. Encouraging the followers is realized by increasing self-confidence (Liden et al. 2008:167).

Leadership is a means of coordination which helps to solve problems related to collaboration, sharing of sources, decision-making related to planning and fulfilling group tasks. The leader tries to make the followers gain benefit as a highly harmonious and coordinated group by serving to his/her followers (Gillet 2011:231).

Servant leaders can also be effective in determining ethical reasoning level and ethical/unethical behaviors of the followers in establishing ethical organization climate and ethical culture (Reed et al. 2011:7).

1.4.4.12   Trainer Leadership

The opinion that decision making stage about what the followers can and cannot do depends on their individual intelligence can be considered as an element which accelerates transition from a manager to trainer leader. Today's leaders undertook important roles in developing facilitating, leading, increasing potentials of the followers and display of their creative aspects rather than individually being involved in events. Trainer leadership can be defined as inviting employees to work, assigning them tasks and responsibility and enabling them to learn a lesson from their experience (İnce et al. 2004:441).

1.4.4.13   Spiritual Leadership

Increased use of internet in business life, excessive satisfaction due to fast access to knowledge, increase of stress causing factors, fast consumption, widespread mechanized structure, the feeling of loneliness experienced by individuals and isolation from the society are the factors which gave rise to spiritual leadership (Baloğlu and Karadağ 2009:173).

Spiritual leadership aims to reach higher levels of organization commitment and efficiency by forming vision and strategy and conducting works to perform individual and team based strengthening (Fry et al. 2005:836).

The conclusions of this type of leadership can be summarized as the followers' satisfaction of the tasks they perform, be at peace with themselves and others and high self-confidence (Serinkan 2008:157).

Future of the organization depends on spiritual leader's determination to detect and solve problems (Fry and Slocum Jr. 2008:93).

Spiritual leaders reveal power to live inside their followers, seek to find the answers to their search for meaning, implement servant leadership in a sense, try to meet the expectations of the followers and make effort for personal development of their followers. These types of leaders have certain traits such as feeling affection, assigning authority, creating value and giving importance to intuition (Kesken and Ayyıldız 2008:746).

The followers don't only have material expectations in working environment. Material rewards satisfy a person only at a certain degree and therefore, the duty of a leader is to hold the followers in high regard and to increase effectiveness and efficiency by creating the sense of belonging (Baloğlu and Karadağ 2009:173).

1.4.4.14 Authentic Leadership

It is not an easy task to lead a small or large organization. Complexity of twenty-first century companies required new leaders. There is a particular need for leaders who design resistant organizations, motivate the followers, create superior customer services and add value to the shareholders in the long term. In short, there is a need for authentic leaders, which is a new type of leadership that will save the organizations from current leadership crisis (George 2003:9).

These types of leaders make decisions without consulting their followers, centralize all authority and manage by creating absolute obedience and fear (Özgen and Yalçın 2006:180–181).

Research on ethical aspect of leadership laid the basis for the emergence and development of the concept of authentic leadership. Authenticity is a concept attributed to the leader by the followers and refers to honesty of the leader firstly to himself/herself rather than to his/her followers (Ünnü 2009:1263).

Authentic means original and not imitated. An authentic leader is aware of how his/her behaviors and thoughts are perceived by the individuals around him/her; know the firstly his/her and later their followers' strong and ethical aspects; recognize the atmosphere of the workplace; have a high level of self-confidence; have optimism and can easily solve his/her problems (Kesken and Ayyıldız 2008:737).

While some authors suggested that authentic leaders support their followers by giving autonomy to their followers and thus create a positive impact on their followers, while some others reported that authentic leaders motivate their followers through ethical issues (Walumbwa et al. 2010:901).

Authentic leadership is considered as a combination of transformational and ethical leadership or as addition of ethical leadership traits to transformative leadership style. An authentic leader is aware of his/her personality, emotions and behaviors; guide the followers through a series of values or high moral standards; are regarded as honest and can be transparent in their actions who also makes fair and balanced decisions (Walker and Walker 2011:383).

1.4.4.15   Liaises: Faire Leadership

In this type of leadership, the followers are given a goal and they are completely free to achieve the goals though their skills. The basic task of the leader is to supply material and source (Yörük et al. 2011:105).

The biggest disadvantage of liaises-faire leadership is that when there is no strong leader, the group of followers remain uninspected and undirected as a result of which the followers feel depressed and the organization drifts into chaos (Şafaklı 2005:135).

A liaises-faire leader doesn't play an active role in decision-making. The decisions related to the tasks they will perform are made by the followers. In other words, liaises-faire leaders avoid taking responsibility and power. The followers motivate and train themselves (İbicioğlu et al. 2009:6).

It can be stated that this leadership style will be beneficial when there are people who are ready to take and don't avoid responsibility in researches of scientists, professional specialization situations and R&D departments or organizations. As a result, these factors can be called the factors that positively affect selection of liaises-faire leadership (Şafaklı 2005:136).

Chapter 2
Communication

Communication is an indispensable element in human life. It can be stated that communication starts when two people notice each other. Communication has an important role in interaction and agreement of people in social and working life. Similarly, communication has a vital role in cooperation of groups and organizations. On the other hand, the concept of communication gains prominence in interaction of states around the world. It can be stated that communication started at the time human beings appeared on the world and developed throughout the time.

2.1 The Concept of Communication and Its Importance

Various definitions were made for the concept of communication. Some of these definitions are explained below.

The word communication is coined from Latin verb "lammuricore", which means to share. Communication is ensuring an understanding between humans to reach desired aims or to influence behaviors (Yörük and Kocabaş 2003:231).

Communication is the process of transferring data, information and understanding from one person to another. In other words, communication provides transfer of information from one person to another. Thus, a person is informed about a certain subject and the person who received information can use that information in his/her work or in other areas (Koçel 2005:530).

Communication is generally defined as the art of knowing other people and introducing oneself to others. At the end of communication process, a person has the opportunity to know other people and to introduce himself/herself to other people. Thanks to communication, we introduce ourselves to other people and get to know others. Particularly leaders can effectively manage their followers by knowing them well. On the other hand, the followers have information about their leaders by knowing them (Özkalp and Sabuncuoğlu 1990:185).

Communication is the art of sending and receiving messages. In other words, communication is considered as an art and attention is paid to the fact that only

S. Ünsar, *Leadership and Communication*, Contributions to Management Science, 27
DOI 10.1007/978-3-319-05248-9_2, © Springer International Publishing Switzerland 2014

understandable messages by the people can be used in communication. As a result, this art should be learnt and applied well (Budak and Budak 2010a:184).

Communication refers to the activities of dissemination of information gained through right/appropriate method and channels to the related people or departments by the sender using right/appropriate method and channel to achieve the goals and aims of the enterprise more effectively and efficiently. Channels appropriate for messages should be selected to make communication effective (Mirze 2010:154).

Communication process starts and continues when two people notice each other. When two people see each other, everything they do or don't do; say or don't say have a meaning. As a result, there is a meaning in voice, posture, look and facial expression (Cüceloğlu 2002:45–46).

An important factor about communication is that it always takes place between two people: the sender and the receiver. A person cannot realize communication process alone. For example, if there is no one around a victim of accident who fell on a deserted island to hear his/her call for help, there will be no communication. In other words, communication is a two-way active process (Davis 1984:504).

A healthy communication process is required for humans to know and understand each other better; for more effective and efficient performance of duties in an organization and solving problems better. Causes of problems can only be found at the end of a good communication (Güney et al. 2007a:43).

When communication is the case, one first thinks of verbal communication. However, communication can take place in different forms. For example, let's think of two 12-year-old boys. One committed a crime while the other one is a boy who should be taken as a model. When these two boys see a policeman in uniform while playing a game in the street, a communication process will be experienced for both boys. However, the message will be different for each. As a result, the situation of people and their perception style might affect communication (Kolasa 1979:319).

Like in all social systems, communication is an important process for the people. The fact that communication is the principle tool for transfer of information in our era is a reason for the increased importance given to communication. In other words, this century is called as the information age. Emergence of information which named the century as an indispensable factor and its transmission to the environment can only take place by communication process. In other words, the way of sharing information is possible through communication (Tutar and Altınöz 2003:113).

Organizational communication can enable a harmonized performance by the people and departments through integration of the employees. Continuation of activities lay the basis for problem solving and formation of creativity. In rapidly changing environmental conditions of the globalizing world, communication enables adaptation to new conditions by rendering an effective information flow (Eroğlu and Sunel 2003:179).

Main aim of communication process is to provide interpersonal interaction. Effective communication means application of the ideas and emotions sent by the source by the receiver in such a way to serve to the expectation and aim of the source. In this respect, communication can be considered as a situation that orientates humans to a certain behavior (Barkan and Eroğlu 2004:115).

Communication in organizations is the principle factor of implementation of decisions in the desired manner. It can be stated that communication in organizations has a strategic character in provision of information used by the management in decision-making; accurate perception and implementation of decisions by human resources; promoting organizational commitment through motivation and job satisfaction; reducing stress and conflict; effectiveness; efficiency and increasing profitability. Leaders can implement numerous subjects of organizational behavior and can make their employees more effective thanks to communication (Özmutaf and Çelikli 2010:2843).

2.2   The Factors Playing a Role in Communication Process

Basic communication process consists of many important elements. These elements are the sender (source), message (information/news), noise, channel, receiver and feedback. The effectiveness and success of communication process can only be possible by complete and accurate performance of the duties of the mentioned elements. These elements are explained below (Megep 2007:4–8; Barker 1990:10–12) (Fig. 2.1).

2.2.1   Sender (Source)

Sender is the person who sends the message and codes the message. In other words, sender is the person who starts communication. Therefore, the sender should be a reliable, knowledgeable, recognized person who knows how to code the message. In other words, the sender can be considered as a spark that starts a big fire (Özgen 2003:101). The sender forms a message through his/her past experiences, perception, thoughts and emotions (Barker 1990:10).

To reach the receiver, the sender firstly codes the emotion, thought and information the communication will convey using language. When correct coding is not performed to protect the essence, the emotion or information will reach the receiver in a different manner; or it will not reach at all. The language of verbal or written communication should be understandable by the receiver. The message should be readable in written messages and audible in verbal messages (Çağırcı and Yeğenoğlu 2007:34).

Interpersonal communication makes data exchange between people possible. Appropriateness of the sender is one of the basic assumptions of an effective and efficient communication. If the sender does not code his/her message according to the thought and perception skill of the receiver, the only outcome will be a mere noise (Tutar and Altınöz 2003:117).

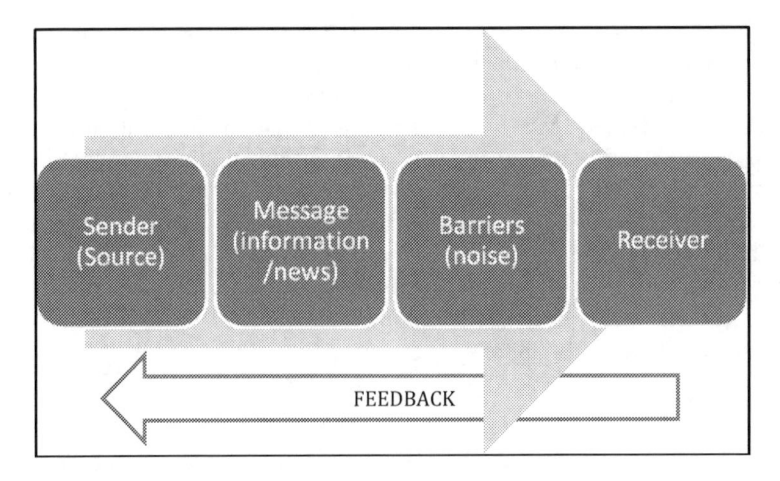

Fig. 2.1 Basic communication process (Daft and Marcic 2006:490)

In communication process, if the sender is considered as the expert of his/her field, it can be an important factor in changing others 'attitudes. For example, a speech delivered by a professor who is experienced in a subject related to economy will have a different impact on the attitudes and thoughts of the receivers (Budak and Budak 2010b:95).

While organizing the message, if the sender uses concrete symbols previously known by the receiver rather than abstract expressions and symbols and if he/she explains certain words and shapes which are not understood by the receiver in detail, it can be stated that communication will be more successful (Topaloğlu and Koç 2003:178–179).

In communication process, the sender should be open to the receiver. Being open means being prepared to negative feedback, contrary opinion, unexpected attitude and undesired respond from the receiver. If the sender becomes open to the receiver, he/she can have the opportunity to take the communication to a desired positive and effective direction without disappointment and despond (Başaran 2000:269–270).

2.2.2   Message (Information/News)

Message is the information the sender shares his/her needs and desires with other people. Effective communication depends on the openness and completeness of the message as much as possible. When the information the message contains is open, it can be easily interpreted or understood. When the message is complete, it contains all necessary information required to establish a common understanding between the sender and the receiver. Sometimes problems might arise in communication process since the sender and the receiver feels equivocality about the content of the message (George and Jones 2012:410).

Message appears after the sender coverts his/her thoughts into codes in appropriate conditions and time using effective symbols. In fact, the message can be considered as a physical product of the sender. On the other hand, an effective message depends on various characteristics such as understandability, openness, timeliness, following the suitable path, receiver and sender (Budak and Budak 2010b:99–100).

Message is a structure consisting of the signs which have a meaning in life. The people learn the meanings of the mentioned signs while using them in the socialization process. A message should have certain characteristics such as understandability and openness, sending to the receiver in an appropriate time and following the right path in communication process to be effective (Güney et al. 2007b:277–279).

The messages which are sent without taking into account the conditions and situations of the receiver fail to show the desired effect in the receiver and as a result, no feedback occurs. For this reason, problems might arise in overcoming the problem. Selection of words, softness or hardness of the verbal expression or written text, the way of expression are reflected in the psychology and emotional status of the sender and the receiver tries to understand the sender from the mentioned content (Metin 2011:181–182).

The message is not something expressed; it is something understood. This requires receivers' understanding of what they heard and understood. What the receiver understands can be only a part of the sender. Moreover, it can be something very different from the subject the sender wants to tell. What will determine the quality of communication is what and how much the receiver understands rather than what the sender thinks (Erbaydar 2003:49).

Accurate perception and understanding of the content of the message by the receiver depends on the following characteristics (Tutar 2003:52):

(a) The message should be open enough to express what the sender wants from the receiver.
(b) The message should follow the most appropriate channel.
(c) The message should be understandable both in terms of form and content.
(d) The message should remain between the source and the receiver without interfering with different people and stages.

The messages are not only formed by the people; there are also messages produced by each environment or place we enter. For example, it can be a pedestrian pavement we walk on, a bank office we go to deposit money or a tax office we visit to pay our taxes. The palaces of the rulers throughout the history were designed to show their power and strength (Cüceloğlu 2002:53).

2.2.3   Barriers (Noise)

Everything that is added to the message between the sender and the receiver without the desire of the sender (against the will of the sender) is considered as the concept of barrier (noise). The thing that delays, damages or even disrupts communication process is a noise (Yılmaz 2003:20).

Barriers or noise can be analyzed in three categories which are physical barriers caused by a problem in sensory organs and the disruptions in communication channels; social psychological (personal) barriers related with the previous experience and past of the receiver which might cause the message to be interpreted differently and the semantic barriers which arise due to failure of accurate/ effective coding of the though handled in communication (Budak and Budak 2010b:102–104).

In communication process, the messages sent by the sender generally do not reach the receiver completely without being subject to loss of meaning. Often differences occur between the sent and perceived messages. The degree of the difference shows the barriers encountered in organizational communication. As the barriers increase, the efficiency of communication decreases. The mentioned barriers result from the deficiency of organizational structure or personal characteristics (Şimşek and Altınkurt 2009:2).

Selection of appropriate channel in communication process enables the message to be accurately and completely transmitted. The situations such as the developments in communication technology and lack of adaptation to these developments by the organizations; inadequate communication channels and carrying a burden exceeding the capacity prevent communication process (Elgünler and Fener 2011:36).

2.2.4   Channel

Channel is the techniques, methods and tools carrying the messages the sender sends to the receiver in line with his/her aims and objectives (Deryakulu 1992:789).

When a presenter is on the radio, as he/she is physically unseen, communication performance might be low; however communication performance will be high when he/she is on TV alive. Appearance of a person can easily affect prestige of the message. For example, when we go to a circus, the clowns are expected to paint their faces and wear appropriate costumes. However, if they get on the stage in normal suits, their performance might be effective. No matter which communication channel is used, the channel that is most appropriate for the message should be selected (Barker 1990:11).

We can talk about formal and informal communication channels in organizations. Formal channels involve top to bottom, and bottom to top means of communication which were previously determined by formal rules. On the other hand, informal communication channels are those that appear by themselves which were not determined by formal rules (Ertürk 2009a:161).

Organizations are based on formal communication channels. On the other hand, both the needs of employees and occasional failures in formal communication channels orientate the employees to informal communication. Informal communication channels are underestimated or even tried to be prevented. However, both channels can be used to achieve organizational goals (Atak 2005:59).

Informal communication channels in an organization support the managers to easily perform their tasks by transmitting information or news in the organization faster than formal channels. On the other hand, if information communication channels are not inspected, they might cause nonfulfillment of tasks, reduced morale among employees and lack of job satisfaction (Solmaz 2006:574).

Message is sent through a channel and the channel carries the message. The channel can be a formal report, telephone call, e-mail message or a face-to-face meeting (Daft and Marcic 2006:489). Telephone is a limited mean in verbal interviews due to factors such as increased or decreased intonation, sound level and stress (Fiske 1990:20).

As long as there is no compulsory condition, the message should be sent to the receiver through known and used channels; conventional means of communication should be made formal communication order through organization arrangements. On the other hand, if the message reaches the receiver though an inappropriate channel, its effectiveness will decrease and the relationship between the sender and receiver can be inadequate (Erdoğan 1997:287).

Selection of appropriate channel in communication involves the appropriateness of the channel that will be selected according to the content of the message. For example, a highway which is built with superior techniques is appropriate for cars however it cannot be suitable for the use of a plane. Therefore, selection of an appropriate channel for each message is important for the quality of communication (Tutar 2003:56).

It can be stated that mass communication devices and five sense organs can have the properties of a channel. Research on this subject revealed that if message is sent from different channels, they have different impacts on the receivers. It was observed that written channels were more successful if the message is not complicated and comprehensive. It was reported that looking at the written message was an advantage when the receiver gets confused (Yüksel and Bir 2005:12).

2.2.5 Receiver

Receiver refers to the person (manager or other employees in the organization), group (formal or informal), organizational department (various offices, branches, divisions etc.) or computer the message is intended to be sent (Ertürk 2009a:160).

Receiver is one of the important elements of basic communication process. The receiver is the person for whom the message is sent and who is tried to be influenced. Depending on the content of the message, the receiver will either have information, use that information or behave for a certain goal. Communication process ends when the receiver accurately perceives the content of the message sent by the sender (Koçel 2010:529).

If the receiver perceives the content of the message differently from the content formulated by the sender, communication fails. While decoding the content and attributing it to a certain meaning, he/she makes an evaluation according to his/her expectations. The success of the receiver in communication depends on objective and unprejudiced analysis of the content of the message (Budak and Budak 2010b:101).

While the sender makes effort to form the message, the receiver makes effort to evaluate and interpret the message at optimum level (Cüceloğlu 1992:73).

It can be stated that, during communication process, emotional state and psychological structure of the receiver play an important role in accurate perception of the message (Efil 2010:197).

Certain characteristics of the receiver such as socio-cultural characteristics, subject of communication, experience and mastership in communication might have positive or negative impacts on communication (Topaloğlu and Koç 2003:181).

In a comprehensive study which aimed determine the extent of understanding the message sent by top managers to their subordinates, it was found that vice managers understood 75 %; inspectors understood 56 %; managers understood 40 %; foremen understood 30 % and the employees who realized the production understood 20 % of the message accurately. An overall analysis of this study reveals that probability of accurate understanding of messages decreased from top to bottom in hierarchical structure (Başaran 2000:279).

2.2.6 Feedback

Feedback refers to informing the sender about he/she received the message and what he/she understood about the content of the message after receiving and evaluating it. Thanks to feedback, the sender learns whether the message is sent to the receiver and has an idea about whether to change the content of the message. If the receiver could fully understand the content of the message, the sender can detect the communication stage which cause this failure and might prevent emergence of the same mistake in the next process. In other words, feedback can be considered as the guarantee of proper and effective communication process (Eren 2007:359). If the message sent by the sender is not understood by the receiver or if there is missing information, this is called negative feedback; if the message is fully understood, this is called positive feedback (Barker 1990:12).

Communication is one-way without feedback; it is becomes two-way with feedback. Feedback strongly assists effectiveness of communication because it enables to understand whether the receiver can correctly interpret the message (Daft 1991:436).

Perhaps the most important impact of feedback is that it develops correct understanding in communication process. On the other hand, feedback also affects employees' performance. Increased feedback (providing timely and constant feedback) can improve work performance. In conclusion, the situation of being good as a whole and job satisfaction can be realized at maximum level (Barker 1990:60–61).

The concept of feedback is also used as an accumulation of knowledge to depict functionless, defects, negative situation, in other words, system problems of the organization, deficiencies and defects of the produced products in terms of quality and number. On the other hand, feedback should also include developments and achievements in organization activities (Başaran 2000:281).

The sender will see the reaction of the receiver and make necessary changes in the content of the message thanks to feedback. Feedback is defining the received message. While making feedback, the benefits both the receiver and the sender expect from communication should be taken into account. As a result, communication barriers will be eliminated. On the other hand, appropriate feedback from managers to make the employees more effective and efficient will motivate the employees (Eroğlu and Sunel 2003:198–199).

Time constraint, parasites, noise etc. negative factors caused by communication channels can always increase the risk of changing the message in terms of content and meaning. Although feedback is considered as a situation that increases costs and causes loss of time, it can provide various advantages in terms of transmitting the message to the receiver without losing content, providing an effective role in organization and starting a dialogue that leads to proximity among people (Şimşek et al. 2008:162).

2.3 Communication Models

In this section, some of communication models developed by scientists to establish proper and effective communication were analyzed and the models were explained in general terms.

2.3.1 Shannon and Weaver's Model of Communication

In this model, the first rule of effective communication is considered as the perception of the message sent by an information source by the destination as desired by the source. This model has a linear line and lacks feedback. It is important that the messages are not disrupted due to a noise in the surrounding for the effectiveness of communication (Öztürk 2006:37).

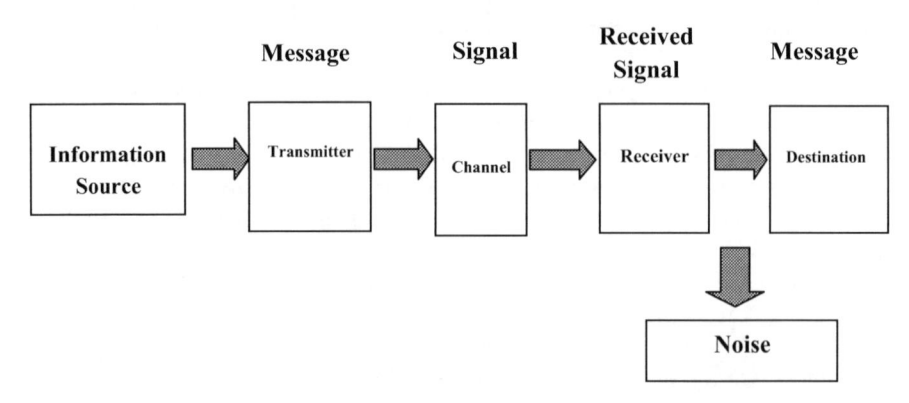

Fig. 2.2 Shannon and Weaver's model of communication (Gökçe 2002:9–11)

As indicated in Fig. 2.2, the model consists of five functions to be fulfilled which are information source, transmitter (transmitting media), message, receiver and destination/receiver and one unfunctional disruptive source noise factor. In the first step of this model, information source selects an appropriate message and sends it to the receiver over the existing communication channel. The receiver does the reverse of the source (Gökçe 2002:9–11). At the first step of this communication method, certain undesired disturbance might be added to the signal. These changes in the signal are termed as noise (Çalışkan 2009:29).

In this model, there are three types of noise that prevents communication process (Polat and Kırıkkaya 2004:4):

(a) Neuro-physical noise: Noise that occur due to sight, audio and speaking problems of the sender or the receiver.
(b) Psychological noise: Psychological noise in the sender or the receiver.
(c) Physical noise: Noise in communication channel that distracts communication.

2.3.2 Laswell Communication Model

As indicated in Fig. 2.3, the act and process of communication are tried to be determined after taking and evaluating most appropriate answers to the questions "Who says what to whom in which channel with what effect?" (Ulutaşdemir 2007:38).

The question "who?" in the figure involves communication or control research; the question "says what?" involves content analysis; the question "in which channel?" involves the media; the question "to whom?" involves audience and finally the question "with what effect?" involves effect research (Gökçe 2002:12).

Fig. 2.3 Laswell communication model (Onur Çoban, Lasswell Modeli, (http://www.onurcoban.com/2011/09/lasswell-modeli.html)

2.3.3 Aristotle's Communication Model

Aristotle defined communication as the art and skill of influencing the listeners by a speaker in the way he/she desires (Akyurt 2009:17). As indicated in Fig. 2.4, Aristotle model involves source, message and listener. In this model, which involves recognized philosopher Aristotle's mode of instructing to his students, one-way communication is used. In this model, the source and the listener are involved indirect communication. In Aristotle model, the listeners are not expected to make a feedback to the message sent from the source (Avcı 2009:12). It can be stated that this model is actually more appropriate for public (general) speaking rather than personal speeches (Narula 2006:25).

Berlo model is often referred to as SMCR model. The name of the model comes from the first letters of the words source, message, channel and receiver (Moore and Dwyer 1994:91–92). Berlo defines his model as a photograph instantiation of the process rather than a cinema film. He reported that an inevitable one-way effect is the case in photograph instantiation and that information moved from source to the receiver. On the other hand, in a cinema film, there is a reciprocal exchange of information between the source and the receiver (Bordenave 2006:421). In this model which was developed by David Berlo, various elements of communication process are explained. As indicated in Fig. 2.5, this model consists of four elements which are source, message, channel and receiver. There are five different channels for each of these four elements. In this model, the element of effect was accepted for the first time. Berlo reported that positive or negative effect of message on the listeners can be formed through effect (result) analysis (Narula 2006:31).

It can be stated that Berlo evaluated human communication as a machine communication. Berlo stated that many problems in interpersonal communication can be solved by using right and appropriate messages. Vagueness of the functions in communication process and lack of feedback are among the limitations of Berlo model (Rosenhauer 2007:130).

2.3.4 Wendel Johnsons Communication Model

The model proposed by Johnsons explains complicated process of communication. Johnsons stated that communication will be more effective when a closer relationship is established with the outer world. Most important contribution of this model to communication models are interpersonal interaction and content (contextual)

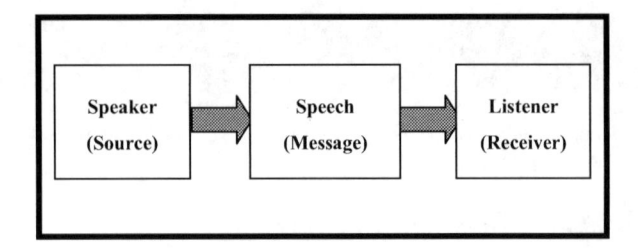

Fig. 2.4 Aristo communication model (Avcı 2009:12)

Source	Message	Channel	Receiver –(Results)
Communication Skills	Elements	Seeing	Communication Skills
Knowledge	Structure	Hearing	Attitudes
Knowledge	Content	Smelling	Knowledge
Social system	Treatment	touching	Social system
Culture	Code	Tasting	Culture

Fig. 2.5 Berlo communication model (Narula 2006:31)

elements. These elements were later developed by different scientists (Narula 2006:29–30).

Johnsons was not interested in attitudes, social situations, speaker skills, or message organization. He studied to define basic elements of communication. In this model, communication is not one-way. Source and receiver can reciprocally and constantly change roles. In other words, the source can sometimes be the receiver and the receiver can sometimes be the sender. Considering physical and psychological elements of verbal communication, it can be stated that this model is advantageous in reciprocal communication (Bettinghaus 2004:23).

2.3.5 Gerbner Model

The model was developed by George Gerbner. In this model, while message is associated with reality, communication process is considered as a process consisting of transmitting and perception dimensions (Gökçe 2002:13).

In this model, Gerbner mentioned the following elements (Berger 1995:14):

1. when
2. someone
3. perceives a situation

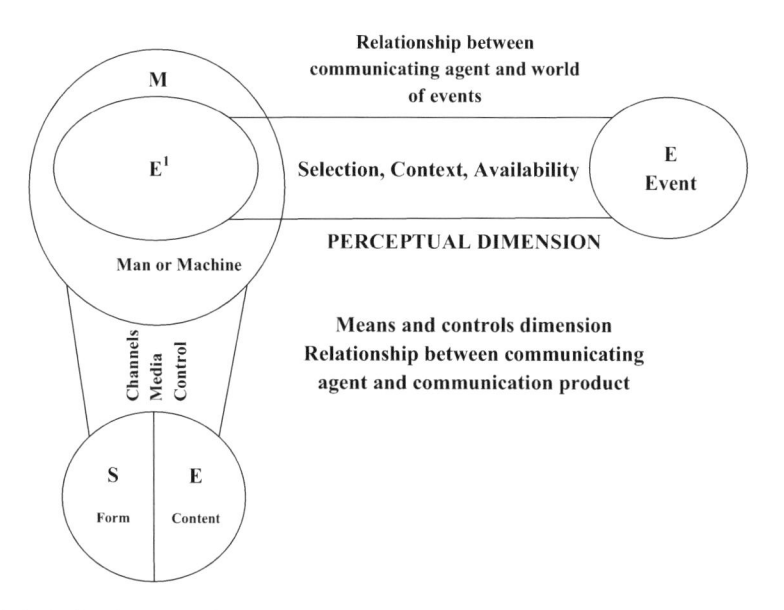

Fig. 2.6 Gerbner's communication model (Gökçe 2002:14)

4. and reacts to it
5. he/she prepares a suitable material
6. using certain tools
7. in this case
8. and reaches some conclusions
9. by sending contents
10. with certain from and content

This model, which was developed by Gerbner in 1956, can be considered as a social and dynamic process. A person perceives a case and the perceived case is an output of the perception activity. Gerbner explained the way message is perceived, difference in perception and characteristics of perception. According to Gerbner, the interaction between the form and content is dynamic rather than static (Usluata 1994:33). The functioning of the model developed by Gerbner is presented in Fig. 2.6.

2.3.6 Newcomb Communication Model

Newcomb developed the model by applying a social system consisting of two people and their interactions to Heider's equilibrium model. Instead of equilibrium, he used the concept of symmetry. He made reference to a qualified order within a social system. Newcomb defined the concept of symmetry as the orientation of A and B to X (Perry 2002:60).

Newcomb reported that continuation of simultaneous orientation of at least two people to themselves and to the objects around them is the most important function

Fig. 2.7 Newcomb
communication model
(Thomlison, http://faculty.
evansville.edu/dt4/301/
primer301.html)

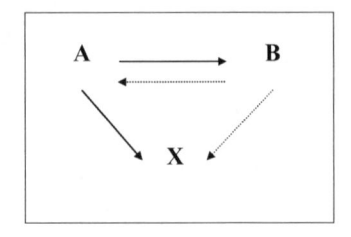

of communication process. According to Newcomb, communication is a learned situation against stress. As a result, more communication behavior is shown in situations of lack of equilibrium and vagueness. As a result, communication is regarded as a situation that provides equilibrium (Gökçe 2002:16).

The model is presented in Fig. 2.7. As indicated in the figure, A and B are both the sender and the receiver. They might be individuals, manager, union, government or human. X is a part of their social environment. ABX is a system and have independent internal relationships. If A changes, then B and X will also change. If A will change its relationship with X, this time B will change its relationship with X or A (Fiske 1990:31).

If A and B are good friends and if X is an object or a person very well known by A and B, then A and B's having the same attitudes towards X will be of great importance. For example, if Can likes rock music a lot, and if Erol doesn't listen to this type of music, Can will try to make Erol like this music or Erol will try to make Can give up listening to rock music. At the end, both of them will continue to be dominant in communication (Bıçakçı 1998:67).

2.3.7   Westley and Mac Lean Communication Model

It can be stated that this model is still used today. In this model, feedback factor is emphasized and the relationship between the elements of mass communication process is explained. Mass communication constitutes an important part of a large social system (Fourie 2007:225). In this model, X symbolizes many thoughts, object, event and human which are present in the outer environment and can be termed as stimulant. On the other hand, component A is the social system or personality which determines and sends messages for a certain goal. C detects the information needed by B and converts them into symbols with a shared meaning. Then C sends them to B through the tool or channel. The messages detected by C can reach a certain goal or might not have any goal. On the other hand, component B can be a group, person or a whole social system. It is one person, a group or a whole social system. The model is presented in Fig. 2.8 (Yüksel 2002:7).

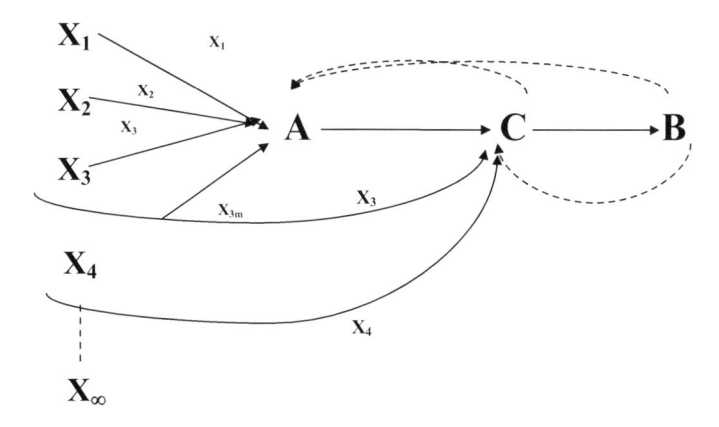

Fig. 2.8 Westley and Mac Lean communication model (McKeown 2005:44)

2.4 Types of Communicaton

There are various types of communication in daily life and business life. The concepts of non-verbal, verbal and written communication are explained below.

2.4.1 Non-Verbal Communication

Non-verbal communication is an effective type of communication which is used to support what we want to say to another individual. Non-verbal communication process occurs with physical behaviors and movements of the individual without the function of speaking. In other words, non-verbal communication involves elements such as facial expressions of the speaker such as grimacing and frowning, intonation and distance between the source and the receiver during communication. The expression that the way we say something to an individual is as important as what we transfer to them indicates the power and importance of non-verbal communication (Paksoy 2002:133).

In a previous study it was shown that facial expression was more effective than verbal communication. For example, think of an employee who says "good morning" to his/her manager at the office. The manager also says "good morning" with a cold expression and in fact ignoring to look at employee's face. That employee can have negative emotions and lose motivation due to this situation. Emotions such as fear, anger, tiredness and joy can also be transferred to the other party in a stronger and more effective manner via non-verbal communication (Megep II 2007:12).

Elements such as distance, arm, hand and head movements, body posture, intonation, eye contact, averting eyes and the posture of the individual according to others are important during the conversation. Environmental communication is related to the subject the individual perceives and interprets from the outer world.

For example, factors such as dressing style, perfume, necklace, use of jewelry, furniture involving artificial elements and the natural world, temperature, music, light, smell are as important as other elements in communication (Erkuş and Günlü 2009:11).

In a study carried out on students about non-verbal communication, it was observed that non-verbal communication skills of teacher significantly contributed to students' comprehension of verbally instructed course. On the other hand, in another study it was found that teacher's smiling while giving the lecture had a significant impact on motivation and concentration of the students (Yavuz and Yüce 2010:227).

Watching each other and reaching judgment without uttering a word is possible by non-verbal communication. Non-verbal communication can make individuals to decide about individuals they did not know before; it also determines the quality and direction of relationships bilaterally for the individuals who knew an individual before (Gürgen et al. 2005:92).

2.4.2   Verbal Communication

It can be stated that verbal communication is the most effective and efficient types of communication. Instead of only listening to the message, perception and evaluation of body movements which explain the aim of the speaker by the listener will make the communication more healthy (Can et al. 1999:232).

Verbal communication refers to transfer of impressions, emotions, design and thoughts of an individual to the receiver verbally. In other words, using verbal communication, functions such as reading poems, singing songs, instructing a course and conversation can be realized (Saraç 2006:3).

Verbal communication consists of face-to-face communication, communication for a certain group, and telephone calls. In this communication type, people receive immediate feedback and are fervent. It was reported that managers generally prefer verbal communication to other types of communication. On the other hand, verbal communication has some drawbacks such as difficulty of recording, ignoring necessary details, loss of time and selection of words (Şahin 2007:88).

Individuals create words while using verbal communication. Similar to differences and similarities in using words, there are also reactions to the words. Words are used as a means to control other people's one's own behaviors. The clearest aspect of this speaking tool is that it has a social aspect. Humans explain their goals, thoughts and emotions to other people through language and speaking (Tekarslan et al. 2000:177).

Verbal communication is generally used by the managers who pare most of their time to speaking. Telephone calls, individual interviews and holding meetings are the most commonly used means of communication used by the managers in verbal communication. The managers also make use of verbal communication in transferring historical background of the organization, values of organizational culture, organizational myth and stories and mission and vision of the organization to their employees (Akıncı 1998:114–115).

In an enterprise if messages go through more than one stage, the content of the message can be changed or disrupted and therefore this can be considered as a disadvantage of verbal message (Paksoy 2002:132).

2.4.3 Written Communication

Invention of writing was such as outstanding event that since it enabled humankind to keep record of the events in social life, it is regarded as the start of history. Therefore it can be stated that the invention of writing makes a significant advantage and contribution to keeping written records of social events (Bingham et al. 2010:16).

Written communication, which started with the invention of writing in historical process, used stone, papyrus, tablet and other objects. Various tablets found in Iraq, Egypt, Mesopotamia and Iran throughout history contained information on various subjects ranging from social and economic life (Bıçakçı 1998:37).

Thanks to cuneiform script developed by the Sumerians, it became possible to write holy stories, agreements, full sentences, laws and many other documents. As a result, it became possible to keep record of and save many works in daily life (McNeill 2008:39).

Written communication is a form of communication which uses paper and other electronic tools. Written communication in enterprises consists of reporting, memo writing procedure and electronic letter. In written communication process, control can be on the sender; however the communication might not be fast. This communication type is mostly preferred in conditions when immediate feedback is not necessary and when there are more than one receiver (Öztürk and Ünlücan 2001:197).

If the messages are desired to be effective and permanent in organizations, using written communication can be advantageous. On the other hand, as the message sent moves by passing through many stages, written content of the message can increase the quality of communication. In addition, written message is important in terms of giving responsibility to the employee for the management and organization (Sabuncuoğlu and Tüz 2001:84).

Notice board, brochures, bulletins, written reports, enterprise newspaper and handouts can be shown as examples of written communication tools. On the other hand, the disadvantages of written communication includes following a hierarchical structure, causing excessive use of stationary, wrong perception of the message by the receiver (Gürsel et al. 2003:47).

2.5 Body Language

The communication in which messages are sent non-verbally without writing only by using certain facial expressions and some body movements is called body language. It can be stated that this communication has many important results (Koçel 2010:537).

In a study carried out to determine to extent words, body language and intonation effects communication process, it was found that

- Words were effective at 7 %
- Intonation was effective at 38 %
- Body language was effective at 55 %

These results reveal that, rather than what we want to say, how we say is important. In other words, it shows the importance of body language (Mısırlı 2003:47).

2.5.1 Elements of Body Language

Elements of body language are gestures and mimes, eye contact, distance and posture. General information on the elements of body language is given below (A.Ü.P.D.R.M. *Beden Dili, http://www.pdrm.anadolu.edu.tr/b/bedendili.pdf*).

2.5.1.1 Gesture and Mimes

In Ancient Greece, theatres were designed to allow the audience to easily hear what was said on the stage. However, since the auditoriums were very large, the audience sitting in the back most rows could not see the play very clearly. For this reason, the actors were wearing various masks which showed their mimes and the roles they played. The masks were double-sided; one side was happy while the other side was sad. During the play the actor turned the mask and continued to act accordingly (Bingham et al. 2010:225).

Various facial expressions in human face due to the use of facial muscles are called mimes. Movement of head, hands, arms, fingers, mimes or the body during the speaking process is called gesture. Gestures can mostly replace speaking language. Holding the fist up to excite the audience by a speaker addressing to a crowded group is a good example to gesture (Kasım 2009:221).

During a conversation, people try to assess the mimes of the other person and to reach certain information about him/her; they can also send positive or negative messages with their mimes. On the other hand, in a study it was reported that two people in a closed room can produce 5,000 units of nonverbal messages in a second (Yüksel 2005:160).

Thanks to gestures and mimes, emotions and thoughts of a person are supported and made concrete. Gestures and mimes are divided into two groups which are principle and secondary ones. Principle gestures and mimes are further divide into three sub-categories which are schematic gestures and mimes; expression gesture and mimes and social gestures and mimes. Movements related to emotions such as surprise, fear, happiness, disgust and anger are the examples of expression gesture and mimes. Smiling to visiting guests despite being tired at home are the examples of social gesture and mimes. On the other hand, movements shown by the panto-mime actors are the examples of schematic gesture and mimes (Yüksel et al. 2005:84).

During a conversation, if a person is angry and tries to conceal this, gestures and mimes of this person can reveal that he/she is angry. In other words, gestures and mimes can be considered as clues that betray our psychological situation (Cüceloğlu 1992:45). On the other hand, while smiling is considered as a positive facial expression in many societies, Koreans prefer to smile under certain conditions and situations (Taylor et al. 2010:67).

It can be stated that, in educational process which is an important function of human resources management, while a subject is explained to a certain group, if gestures and mimes are often used by the educators, this will make the lecture more vivid and will save the lecture from being boring. As a result, it can be stated that gesture and mimes contribute giving lecture (Bilgin et al. 2004:109–110).

2.5.1.2 Eye Contact

On should pay attention to manage eye contact to establish a successful communication. Understanding looks contributes to understanding messages for proper continuation of communication. Eyes are the first region people look at during communication process and influencing each other is closely related to eye contact (Salmış 2011:101).

Eyes in human face are like the windows of a house. Pupils dilate in a dark, and shrink in light. Previous studies revealed that as the level of interest to an object increases pupils dilate as well. In addition, dilated pupils express honesty, sexual or a real information, comfort and relaxation (Gürgen et al. 2005:96).

If pupils are dilated, this is considered as indication of insecurity, hostility, less attention, grudge, stress, fatigue and dissatisfaction. On the other hand, staring or gazing into other person's eyes can cause distress. If the other person does not look into our eyes during speaking, this can arise the feeling of lack of respect (Gürgen et al. 2005:96).

Using eye contact effectively, we can make the other person feel that we give importance and value to that person. For example, while addressing to or listening to a customer, a sales clerk should make eye contact by looking at the eye region without distressing him/her. Otherwise, the customer might think that he/she is not given importance (Yılmaz et al. 2005:36).

During laughing, human face tends to contract upward, however, even in this situation, it is reported that eyes express the real emotion. In other words, eyes cannot conceal the real emotion and feeling; they cannot lie (Tekarslan et al. 2000:194).

2.5.1.3   Distance

Distance is a controllable element of communication. For this reason, using distance in optimum manner both in one-to-one communication and in communication established with a crowded society can contribute to communication. The distance a person keeps with the other person during conversation (standing near or far) is related to emotions to that person (Özbent 2007:275).

People establish communication over four distances which are intimate distance, personal distance, social distance and public distance. Intimate distance refers to 30–35 cm distance in which we allow intimate people we feel close. Personal, sincere distance refers to 40–80 cm distance in which two people knowing each other speak. Social distance varies between 80 cm and 2 m distance. Finally, public distance is the distance which is longer than two meters and it is open to the people we don't know. In other words, the closer and sincere the other people are, the shorter the distance is (Cüceloğlu 1992:38–39).

2.5.1.4   Posture

During communication, one should stand erect and should not slouch. If standing erect is exaggerated, the other person might think that we stand like a bully and might not be contented with this. On the other hand, if the person excessively slouches and droops, the other person might think that we don't really intent to communicate (Mısırlı 2003:55). As we see, like the case in marketing, people should have a proper posture. For example, a sales clerk should meet a customer entering the store in standing position and should stand erect. He/she should not lean on the wall or the table while listening to the customer; he/she should slightly bend forwards and should pay attention to the customer. It can be stated that this attitude shows respect to the customer (Arslan and Bayçu 2006:225).

2.6   Organizational Communication

The concept of communication is important in enterprise management like in social and private life. Enterprises should make production, make profit and grow by using this profit to maintain and continue their existence. Communication plays a vital role during the course of these activities. When we consider enterprises as an organization, there is a need for communication in internal structure of the communication which functions effectively and efficiently. Since organizations consist of more than one department, there is intense communication in and between these departments. While conducting planning, organization, orientation, coordination and inspection functions, managers mostly make use of communication. Interpersonal communication is employed in application of all these functions. Proper functioning of this communication will enable the organization to achieve organizational goals. In this section, organizational communication and sub titles will be explained.

2.6.1 What Is Organizational Communication?

Organizational communication can be defined as various department and elements that constitute the enterprise and enable functioning of the enterprise or to achieve the goals of the enterprise; constant exchange of ideas and information between the enterprise and outer world or as a social structure that enables to build necessary relationships between the departments. As understood from the definition, organizational communication aims to provide production by the enterprise and to achieve organizational goals (Sabuncuoğlu and Tüz 2001:75).

Organizational communications expresses more than daily relationship and interactions of the employees in an enterprise. It points out to a process which is created and shared by the members of the organization through interaction. It can be stated that, the following five basic characteristics should be known to understand and evaluate organizational communication process: (Kaya 2003:119):

(a) Communication includes a symbolic structure,
(b) Communication includes doing business and behavior
(c) Communication takes place between two or more people in a social environment,
(d) Communication has a certain goal,
(e) Communication process is a complex and continuous process which cannot be isolated.

2.6.2 Types of Organizational Communication

Communication used in organizations is divided into two groups: (Gürsel et al. 2003:41);

- Formal communication
- Informal communication

2.6.2.1 Formal Communication

In an organization, if the structure and forms of all communication are determined by the managers and if they are used as they liked, then this structure is called formal communication. In this form of communication it can be stated that the manager or the enterprise owners are in control. Communication takes place via previously determined means and forms of communication (Tutar 2003:124).

Formal communication is divided into four groups which are vertical, horizontal, diagonal and extroverted communication (Ada et al. 2008:490). These groups are explained below.

Vertical Communication

Vertical communication consists of "top to down" and "down to top" communication. In "top to down" communication, there is an information flow the top management to the lowest level. In this form of communication, orders, instructions, procedures, directives, work information, performance evaluation and organizational information are conveyed generally using written communication (Gürsel et al. 2003:42; Mirze 2010:154). For example, as indicated in Fig. 2.9, an order sent from the production manager to a chief working in the atelier can be an example to top to down communication.

This form of communication has certain disadvantages. Firstly, the message might be subject to changes while it is sent to lower levels and can have a different meaning. On the other hand, behaviors of the managers to their subordinates and the trust of subordinates to their managers play an important role in accurate perception of the message (Ada et al. 2008:490).

On the other hand, in "down to top communication" which is the second form of vertical communication, the subordinates transfer information, wishes, suggestions and complaints etc. about the outcomes of the order and instructions previously sent to them to higher level managers. In short, there is a flow of information from subordinates to the managers (Şimşek et al. 2008:167). For example, as indicated in Fig. 2.10, transfer of information and suggestion for a solution about a problem by an engineer working in a project to the project manager can be an example to down to top communication.

After fulfilling a task assigned to them, the subordinates present the results to the higher level in the form of a report. The content of the report can be a completed project or information about the stage of a continuing project. As a result, the employees inform the management about the content and final status of a work. This can also be considered as a feedback towards the managers. Thanks to this form of communication, the managers have positive or negative information about the work. The subordinates can ask their superiors' help by occasionally consulting to them and taking their ideas while making a decision or solving a certain problem.

Fig. 2.9 Top to down
communication

Chief

Fig. 2.10 Down to top
communication

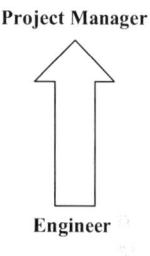

These can be considered as the examples of down to top communication
(Benligiray 2005:139; Gürgen 2005:142).

Horizontal Communication

Horizontal communication is a form of communication which takes place between
the units and people at the same hierarchical level. For example, exchange of
information between human resources manager and marketing manager working
in the same company can be an example of horizontal communication. Horizontal
communication is presented in Fig. 2.11. Establishing coordination between and in
different organizational departments is the most important function of horizontal
communication. Specialization and differentiation caused by excessive division of
labor in modern and huge enterprises made coordination between the departments
important (Can 1999:235).

Horizontal communication is the relationship and interaction that occurs as a
result of cooperation between same-level managers in shared subjects without
taking the order of upper levels (Budak and Budak 2010a:201).

In horizontal communication, rather than leadership traits a person has to
convince other person or people, "persuasion technique" gains prominence. The
person does not directly express a situation that should be done to their colleagues at
the same level. For this reason, he/she tries to persuade them with his/her logical
ideas (Taşçı and Eroğlu 2007:534).

Horizontal communication is particularly important in "learning organizations".
Team members working in these types of organizations constantly solve problems
and search for new ways for problem-solving. Numerous organizations form

Fig. 2.11 Horizontal
communication

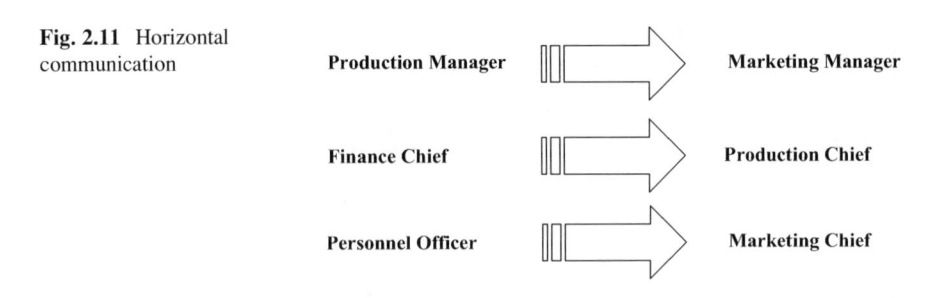

Production Manager ⟹ Marketing Manager

Finance Chief ⟹ Production Chief

Personnel Officer ⟹ Marketing Chief

horizontal communication within special task groups, committees or matrix structures to encourage coordination (Daft and Marcic 2006:506).

Diagonal Communication

Communication used by the departments in different parts of organizations without
using hierarchical channels is called diagonal communication. Diagonal communication is important in terms of eliminating the disadvantages of complex and long
vertical communication and to build an effective cooperation. For example, giving
orders to all employees by a chief without using vertical or horizontal communication channels to eliminate negative situations at the time of or after an earthquake
can be an example to diagonal communication. On the other hand, frequent use of
this form of communication can give rise to the problem of confusion of authority
and therefore one should avoid using this form of communication as a rule as long
as it is not compulsory in organizations (Tutar 2003:130–131 and Sabuncuoğlu and
Tüz 2001:82–83).

Diagonal communication is beneficial as it is fast, effective and efficient.
Widespread use of e-mail made diagonal communication easy. In most organizations, an employee can communicate with another employee or even with a superior
manager without taking organizational working field or level. Today, CEOs of man
enterprises adopt e-mail policy which is called "open inbox". Thanks to this, most
CEOs can communicate with their employees (Robbins and Coulter 2012:413).

It can be stated that diagonal communication is related with the principle of
hierarchical structure which Henri Fayol termed as "Fayol's Bridge". According to
this principle, two superiors working in different departments can normally communicate directly only by informing their superiors (Koçel 2010:219).

A vice manager of an enterprise can want to learn operation properties of a
device which was bought from a foreign country and at the stage of assembly. For
this reason, he/she go beyond official channels and can demand technical data from
an experienced engineer about that device. As a result, diagonal communication
takes place (Arısoy 2007:27).

On the other hand, the concept "MBWA" (Management by Walking Around)
gained popularity in recent years. This concept is classified as formal and informal
communication. In Management by Walking Around, managers freely spend time

with their employees by establishing open connection in production unit, office and social organizations. As a result, the managers learn the existing problems in their source (DuBrin 2012:435). In Management by Walking Around, the manager developed positive direct relationships with the employees and collects information about what has been going around In departments and organizations. Managers become isolated when they fail in Management by Walking Around (Daft and Marcic 2006:509).

Extroverted Communication

Since enterprises are open systems, they have to use extra-organizational communication channels in addition to intra-organizational channels to survive and compete with other enterprises which manufacture in a dynamic and constantly changing environment. There is a considerable amount of data and information flow from outside to the enterprise. Managers evaluate this information and make decisions in various matters; they constantly make changes, improvements and developments in organizational structure, operation and work programs and behavior types (Mısırlı 2003:15). In this communication type, while information about the interior world of the enterprise is sent to the outer world; the enterprise receives information it needs from the outer environment. A letter sent from one enterprise to another is an example to extroverted communication.

2.6.2.2 Informal Communication

In addition to formal communication; the enterprises also have information communication which includes rumors. This communication type is used by intimate employees who know each other very well without the permission of their managers. Information communication is performed face-to-face or using telephone excluding formal communication channels. Through informal communication, individual information and rumors can be disseminated within the organization; social relationships can be developed and enhanced (Akıncı 1998:127).

Informal communication exists due to the limitations of formal communication. In other words, informal communication completes the deficient aspects ıf formal communication. It was found that 75–90 % of information transferred through rumors were correct. In a study carried out on middle level managers, it was reported that informal communication was a better source than formal communication. On the other hand, information is transferred more quickly through rumors. Employees feel more job satisfaction and increased commitment to the organization as a result of making rumors. Effective managers can have information about the problems and anxieties of their employees through informal communication channel (Hamilton 2011:33–34).

2.7 Organizational Communication Tools

In enterprises, various tools are used in communication process. It can be stated that used tools vary according to the structure of communication. In addition, rapid development of communication technology and thus means of communication also changed the means used in enterprises. On the other hand, means of communication can vary according to the person or communication environment to whom the message will be sent. In this chapter, written, verbal and audio-visual means used in communication process were explained.

2.7.1 Means of Written Communication

Various written means of communication are used in organizations. Written means are used due to their permanent nature. A person can forget a given order and therefore he/she can remember that order by checking a written paper or an electronic tool. In addition, an order which is given orally can be forgotten and thus giving a written order might be more effective. Like in the saying "Word is temporary, writing is permanent", it can be stated that giving orders and instructions in writing has a great importance in terms of communication. Written means of communication are divided into four categories which are written reports, company newspaper, manuals, brochures and notice boards.

2.7.1.1 Written Reports

Managers can ask for periodical reports from their subordinates about the final status of a certain task. The managers who read the reports have information about the course of the work and encountered problems. These reports prepared by the subordinates should be issued in a simple and precise language. In addition, they should be complete and accurate (Sabuncuoğlu and Tüz 2001:86).

Reports on an ongoing project and annual activity reports are written documents of this type. After reading and assessing these reports, the managers can make decisions for the future and can implement their own measures if necessary. On the other hand, preparation of written reports by the employees about their opinions or activities lay the basis for strengthening hierarchical relationship. Furthermore, it can be stated that the subordinates who observe that their reports are taken into account by their managers and are used for various activities will have increased job satisfaction, organizational commitment and motivation levels (Kaynak et al. 1998:434).

2.7.1.2 Company Newspaper

Today the majority of enterprises issue a periodical newspaper. The newspapers are issued for intra-organizational and extra-organizational communication. They are issued bimonthly, monthly, semi-monthly or weekly. In today's globalizing world, more than three hundred millions of company newspapers are estimated to be issued. Company newspapers contain news about general matters, social activities, current issued about working life, security, various news and information about the services of the organization (Gürgen et al. 2005:147).

Thanks to company newspaper, one can have information about junior employees, retired personnel, the deceased, the personnel who quit work, the personnel who were rewarded for their achievements, happy days and social and economic structure of the enterprise. These newspapers should use a clear and understandable language and should take the opinions and suggestions of the employees, which will increase effectiveness and readability of the newspaper (Kaynak et al. 1998:430).

2.7.1.3 Manuals

The elements and relationships in the formal structure which emerge in enterprises following the completion of organizational process are tried to be explained by a material called manual (Karalar et al. 2006:29).

Organizational manual is a means of communication which mostly use writing rather than pictures and contains a lot of numbers. They are prepared to help junior employees to adapt to the working environment in a short time (Ada et al. 2008:492). It can be stated that these books are occasionally used to gain information about the problems a junior employee encounters in the working life.

2.7.1.4 Brochures and Notice Boards

Brochures and signboards are written paper or electronic devices which are hanged in areas mostly visited and easily visible by the employees in the workplace. The brochures which are prepared to draw the attention and interest of employees contain pictures and lines. Hanging various visuals and written papers on notice boards, the employees are informed about a subject. On the other hand, digital devices and LCD televisions with an electronic screen which can be mounted on the wall are increasingly used in work places and offices in recent years. Thanks to these means of communication, office workers have the opportunity to learn the latest information and news about the company or the business life from these electronic devices (Budak and Budak 2010a:203–204).

2.7.2   Verbal Communication Tools

Various means of verbal communication are used in enterprises. Verbal communication is preferred if the given order will be fulfilled in a short time. The biggest disadvantage of verbal communication is the possibly of misunderstanding of the sent message. Conferences and meetings are the examples of verbal communication.

2.7.2.1   Conference

Conference is a one-way means of communication which allows for the transfer of information and ideas to a large audience. If the subject of the conference is not interesting enough, it might fail to achieve the desired goal. In addition, since one-way communication is the case in conference, it prevents feedback. Audio and visual tools are used today to increase effectiveness of conference and to enhance attention of the audience. In addition, conference is preferred to increase knowledge and manners of the employees from all departments on condition that they are held on various subjects (Sabuncuoğlu 1998:146, Kaynak et al. 1998:432).

2.7.2.2   Meetings

Meeting is a small group formation, generally consisting of five to ten people which discuss organizational matters that reciprocally affect each other. Meetings are generally held to disseminate information or to find solutions to current organizational problems (Barker 1990:231). Managers build trust and cooperation by face-to-face contact through meetings. Representatives of each department attend the meetings and determine the activities and organizational policies (Mejia and Balkin 2012:266). Meetings with the members of organizations include training and informing the participants; problem solving; monitoring and coordination activities; assignments and formation of social connections between different members of the organization (Mejia and Balkin 2012:423).

2.7.3   Audiovisual Tools

Junior employees can watch images about working conditions, physical structure and production process of the organization using audiovisual tools such as films, DVD or videos. These tools can transfer detailed and important data to the personnel in a permanent manner and in a short time (Kaynak 1998:432). Today's organizations make use of audiovisual tools such as overhead projector, slights, video, projector, tape, compact disc (CD), television and computer (Benligiray 2005:93).

2.8 Organizational Communication Barriers

Organizational communication process contains various barriers which prevent and disrupt communication among people, departments or organizations. The following section will explain these barriers.

2.8.1 Emotion and Perceptions of Employees

Each person has a different personality, background and knowledge level and thus he/she can perceive the same message in a different manner. As a result, the receiver can attribute a different meaning from that of the sender to the related message (Daft and Marcic 2006:514). Excessive emotionality is a significant barrier in effective communication. In emotional decisions, rational and objective thinking processes are generally ignored. A subordinate in a psychology of excessive anger or sadness might perceive a message sent by the manager differently (Robbins and Coulter 2012:409).

2.8.2 Weak Listening

Human body contains two ears and one tongue. This can mean that we should give more importance to listening than speaking. We use one ear to listen and the other to understand (Davis 1984:526). People prefer to speak rather than to listen to other people. As a result of this, they fail to fully understand the message the other person wants to give. There are various ways to be a better receiver or listener. The sender should be given full attention to be a better listener. For example, one should look at the eyes of the speaker and should not interrupt him/her. Weak listening can cause misunderstanding of the message sent by the sender (George and Jones 2012:416).

2.8.3 Wrong Communication Channel

Selecting a channel appropriate for the content of the message will make communication more effective. Selection of a wrong channel can disrupt the meaning of the message. For example, if the message is emotional, face-to-face communication should be used rather than writing. By this way the receiver will perceive the message better. It is highly risky to discuss particularly difficulty matters using electronic mail. In other words, electronic mail is effective only for ordinary messages; however it is disadvantageous in terms of feedback. Therefore, it can be stated that it should not be preferred (Daft and Marcic 2006:514). On the other hand, it might not be appropriate to write a short note for an explanation about an amendment in retirement plans of the employees (Mejia and Balkin 2012:418).

2.8.4 Inappropriate Language (Semantic Barrier)

The language used in structure of a message should be appropriate for the receiver. Particularly semantic factors gain importance at this point. Semantic factor is related to the symbols used while forming the message. A certain symbol can have different meanings for some people; on the other hand certain symbols can have more than one meaning. Imagine that a manager said "Our department should be more productive." The majority of the employees will interpret this sentence accurately meaning working more effectively. However, some of the employees will interpret his message as harder work and longer working hours for the same wage and will show resistance to this message (Koçel 2010:534; DuBrin 2012:444–445).

2.8.5 Excessive Information

Today's employees often complain about excessive information load. According to statistics, 87 % of employees use electronic mail and spare approximately 25 % (107 h) of their working days to electronic mails. Another statistics shows that employees send or receive 150 electronic mails on average every day. On the other hand, excessive information load might be the case also in facsimile, meeting and telephone conversations. The employees ignore, forget or remain indifferent for this excessive information load or they become picky about information selection. They can also stop communication, which causes loss of information and ineffective communication (Robbins and Coulter 2012:409–410).

2.8.6 Time Constraints

While sending a message to the receiver, one should pay attention to check that the receiver has no time constraint. A schedule should be made prior to communication. For example, before making an interview, a statement like "We have a 1 h period for this interview and thus we have to use this time effectively without exceeding it," will help the related person in using time (Tutar 2003:160).

2.9 Leadership and Communication

The ability of establishing good communication with the environment is one of the important qualities of an effective and efficient leader. However, establishing good communication in a certain environment alone does not make a person a leader. Today the masters who are admired in theater and performing arts failed to lead people as a leader despite their perfect communication skills (Baltaş 2001:112).

Success of a leader depends on effectiveness and efficiency of the followers. Therefore, the leader has to establish effective communication with the followers. It can be stated that the success of the leader depends on transferring his/her goals and aims to his/her followers. Furthermore, receiving feedback from the followers is also important. Leadership and communication are indispensable. Can a person who fails establishing communication be a leader? A good leader is the person who transfers high important information to his/her followers using the most appropriate channel. It can be stated that particularly face-to-face communication supported by written texts is the best method. Thus, the follower can have an advantage to check the written text when he/she fails to remember or be sure about a given order (Adair 2004:225).

The leader should have good communication skill which enables exchange of opinions, ideas and information between different departments and organizations to achieve his/her goals and to ensure proper survival of the organization (Yiğit 2002:19).

"Listening" which is an important element of basic communication process, is a principle ability of leadership. If the leaders' don't listen to group members carefully, they cannot detect existing problems. On the other hand, listening given an opportunity for reciprocal speaking. Thus, people understand each other better. A leader should support or encourage his/her subordinate about active listening (DuBrin 2010:358).

Leaders use various methods of communication including diverse channels such as stories, metaphors and informal communication (Daft 2008:263). Historical and contemporary leaders like Reagan, Kings and Jobs gave important messages to their followers using their strong communication abilities.

A study carried out on different workplaces in Turkey found that leaders lacked communication abilities such as empathy, effective listening and feedback. Deficiency of these abilities can be considered as a factor that disrupts proper functioning of enterprises. On the other hand, the enterprises which were aware of the importance of communication provided necessary trainings to their managers and tried to eliminate their lacking abilities (Baltaş 2010:45–46).

A good leader transfers messages to his/her followers after listening to them. In addition, he collects information by asking questions such as How can I help you?" Are our goals appropriate? Are there any barriers? What do you need? Are there and obstacles that hinder you from achieving the goals? (Tekin 2008:117). The leader should first try to understand his/her followers before expecting to be understood.

Bill Hewlett and David Packard founded Hewlett and Packard (HP) company in 1938 in California to produce electronic devices. Both leaders implemented "open door policy" and enabled their employees to discuss personal or business matters with their managers. Thus, the employees had the opportunity to share their opinions and ideas with their leaders (Bhardwaj and Madan 2009:31–32).

Many leaders in industry achieved success using MBWA approach. Thanks to this approach, they established good communication with the employees and encouraged personnel participation. As a result, strong communication was established between the managers and employees (Aamodt 2010:456).

It can be stated that a good leader should have the ability to make empathy for good communication. Previous studies found that leaders had good empathy abilities. Characteristics of a leader such as high social sensitivity, expressing himself/herself to the followers, establishing positive and adaptable communication require the skill of empathy in individuals (Özgen 2003:114).

The leaders motivate and influence the employees to make them show a performance in parallel to previously determined aims and goals using various means of communication. The leaders establish communication with their employees like those between an inspector and a student or a football player and coach. On the other hand, a high number of leaders prevent feedback from employees as they don't want to hear negative information. Despite this, leaders often make decision and planning (Daft 2008:260).

Chapter 3
Leadership and Organizational Communication: A Study in Glass, Textile and Apparel Sectors

3.1 Methodology

Methodology of the study is explained below. This section will explain the aim and significance of the study, assumptions, population and sampling, data collection method and HYPOTHESES of the study.

3.2 Aim and Significance of The Study

This study aimed to determine the relationship between leadership behavior types and communication styles of the managers of the employees working in glass, textile and apparel sectors and socio-demographic variables and leadership behavior types and communication styles of their managers. In addition, another aim of the study was to compare leadership behavior types and communication styles in terms of glass, textile and apparel sectors. Since leadership and communication are among important elements of achieving a success in business life, it is important to determine and analyze leadership behavior types and communication styles of managers in glass, textile and apparel sectors.

3.3 Assumptions

It was assumed that the employees working in glass, textile and apparel sector accurately perceived and answered the questions in the questionnaire.

S. Ünsar, *Leadership and Communication*, Contributions to Management Science, 59
DOI 10.1007/978-3-319-05248-9_3, © Springer International Publishing Switzerland 2014

3.4 Population and Sampling of the Study

Population of the study consisted of glass, textile and apparel enterprises in Turkey. Sampling of the study consisted of glass, textile and apparel enterprises in Thrace Region of Turkey.

3.5 Data Collection Method and Used Statistics

Questionnaire Form in the appendix of the book was used for data collection. The Questionnaire Form consisted of three sections. The first section contained questions to determine socio-demographic characteristics (age, gender, marital status, education etc.) of the employees.

The second section contained "Leadership Behavior Questionnaire" developed by Ekvall and Arvonen (1991:17–26) which was adapted into Turkish by Tengilimoğlu (2005:23–45). The permissions of the mentioned scientists were taken to administer the scales on the employees in three sectors. "Leadership Behavior Questionnaire" was developed to determine three types of leadership behaviors and consists of a total of 36 statements. The statements 1, 2, 4, 7, 10, 13, 16, 19, 22, 25, 28, 31, 32 and 34 aimed to determine employee-oriented leadership behavior; statements 3, 6, 9, 12, 15, 18, 21, 24, 27, 30, 33 and 36 aimed to determine task-oriented leadership behavior, and statements no 5, 8, 11, 14, 17, 20, 23, 26, 29 and 35 aimed to determine change-oriented leadership behavior (Kelez 2008:126). This is a 5-item Likert scale which ranged from Strongly Disagree, Disagree, Undecided, Agree and Strongly Agree. Reliability analysis was performed for Leadership Behavior Scale and reliability coefficient was found to be (Cronbach alpha) = 0.98. In addition, reliability coefficient of employee-oriented leadership behavior sub-dimension was found to be (Cronbach alpha) = 0.96; reliability coefficient of task-oriented leadership behavior was found to be (Cronbach alpha) = 0.95 and reliability coefficient of change-oriented leadership behavior was found to be (Cronbach alpha) = 0.94. These values showed that the scale and its sub-dimensions had high reliability degree.

The third section used "Communication Scale" designed and developed by the researcher by the compilation of literature data (Koçel 2010:526–534; Eren 2003:450–463; Yılmaz 2008:203–204; Yüksel 2005:306; Youssef 2005:54–75; Gürsun 2007:158; Hacıoğlu 2007:67–68). This scale contained 25 statements. It is a 5-item Likert scale ranging from Strongly Disagree, Disagree, Undecided, Agree and Strongly Agree. As a result of factor analysis, the scale was reduced to one dimension under "communication". Similarly, reliability analysis was performed for communication scale and reliability coefficient was found to be (Cronbach alpha)=0.98. This value indicates that the scale has a high reliability degree.

The questionnaires were actively administered to the employees after taking necessary permissions. Following the preparation of the questionnaires, the mentioned enterprises were visited; heads of department were informed about how to fill in the questionnaires and they were then distributed to the employees. Approximately 700 questionnaires were distributed to enterprises. However, a total of 628 questionnaires were evaluated due to mistakes and various unfilled sections in the general of questionnaires. SPSS statistics package program was used to evaluate the questionnaires. Various statistical analyses were applied on the obtained data and data were analyzed and interpreter using the tables. Mann-Whitney U, Kruskal Wallis, Tukey multiple comparison tests were applied on the data. The results were evaluated at a significance level of 0.05 and 0.10.

3.6 Hypotheses of the Study

A total of 11 hypotheses were developed to test according to the aims of the study. These hypotheses are explained below.

HYPOTHESIS-1:

- H_0: There is no significant difference between marital status, leadership behavior types and communication viewpoint of the employees.
- H_1: There is a significant difference between marital status, leadership behavior types and communication viewpoint of the employees.

HYPOTHESIS-2:

- H_0: There is no significant difference between Working Status of Spouses, leadership behavior types and communication viewpoint of employees.
- H_1: There is a significant difference between Working Status of Spouses, leadership behavior types and communication viewpoint of employees.

HYPOTHESIS-3:

- H_0: There is no significant difference between age, leadership behavior types and communication viewpoint of employees.
- H_1: There is a significant difference between age, leadership behavior types and communication viewpoint of employees.

HYPOTHESIS-4:

- H_0: There is no significant difference between seniority, leadership behavior types and communication viewpoints of employees.
- H_1: There is a significant difference between seniority, leadership behavior types and communication viewpoints of employees.

HYPOTHESIS-5:

- H_0: There is no significant difference between gender, leadership behavior types and communication viewpoints of employees.
- H_1: There is a significant difference between gender, leadership behavior types and communication viewpoints of employees.

HYPOTHESIS-6:

- H_0: There is no significant difference between the working sectors, leadership behavior types and communication viewpoint of employees.
- H_1: There is a significant difference between the working sectors, leadership behavior types and communication viewpoint of employees.

HYPOTHESIS-7:

- H_0: There is no significant difference between family income, leadership behavior types and communication viewpoints of employees.
- H_1: There is a significant difference between family income, leadership behavior types and communication viewpoints of employees.

HYPOTHESIS-8:

- H_0: There is no significant difference between place of upbringing, leadership behavior types and communication viewpoints of employees.
- H_1: There is a significant difference between place of upbringing, leadership behavior types and communication viewpoints of employees.

HYPOTHESIS-9:

- H_0: There is no significant difference between educational status, leadership behavior types and communication viewpoint of employees.
- H_1: There is a significant difference between educational status, leadership behavior types and communication viewpoint of employees.

HYPOTHESIS-10:

- H_0: There is no significant difference between educational status of mothers, leadership behavior types and communication viewpoint of employees.
- H_1: There is a significant difference between educational status of mothers, leadership behavior types and communication viewpoint of employees.

HYPOTHESIS-11:

- H_0: There is no significant difference between educational status of fathers, leadership behavior types and communication viewpoints of employees.
- H_1: There is a significant difference between educational status of fathers, leadership behavior types and communication viewpoints of employees.

Table 3.1 Distribution of participants according to gender

Variable	Options	Frequency	fi%
Gender	Female	465	74
	Male	163	26
	Total	628	100

3.7 Socio-Demographic Characteristics of the Participants

Socio-demographic characteristics of the employees who participated in the study are presented below using tables and graphs.

Genders of the employees who participated in the study are presented in Table 3.1 and Graph 3.1. As indicated in the table, of the employees, 74 % were female, 26 % were male. Based on this result, it can be stated that the majority of the employees were female. The fact that females were highly employed in textile and apparel sectors can be considered as the cause of high number of female employees in the present study.

Educational statuses of the employees who participated in the study are presented in Table 3.2 and Graph 3.2. As indicated in the table, of the employees, 57.3 % graduated from high school; 18.8 % graduated from primary school; 11.8 % graduated from secondary school; 10.8 % graduated from 2-year college and 1.3 % graduated from 4-year university. Based on these results, it can be stated that majority of the employees were high school graduates. The fact that high school graduates were preferred more in textile and apparel sectors can be considered as the cause of high number of high school graduate employees in the present study.

Distribution of employees who participated in the study according to their marital status is presented in Table 3.3 and Graph 3.3. As indicated in the table, of the employees, 83.4 % were married; 16.6 % were single. Based on these results, it can be stated that majority of participants were married.

Table 3.4 and Graph 3.4 indicate distribution of the employees who were included in the study according to age groups. As indicated in the table, of the employees, 47–9 % were between the ages of 31–40; 31.2 % were between the ages of 20–30; 20.4 % were between the ages of 41–50 and 0.5 % were at the age of 51 and above. According to these findings, it can be stated that the majority of the employees were between the age of 31–40, which means middle age group.

Distribution of the employees who participate in the study according to seniority levels are presented in Table 3.5 and Graph 3.5. As indicated in the table, of the employees, 53.3 % had 1–10-year seniority level; 37.1 % had 11–20-year seniority level; 9.2 % had 21–30-yar seniority class and 0.3 % had 31 and longer-year seniority level. Based on these results, it can be stated that majority of the employees had 1–10 years of seniority, which is not very long.

Distribution of the employees who participated in the study according to income levels is indicated in Table 3.6 and Graph 3.6. As indicated in the table, of the employees, 86.6 % had an income range of 701–2,200 TL; 8.9 % had an income range of 700 and below; 3.7 % had an income range of 2,201–3,700 TL; 0.6 % had

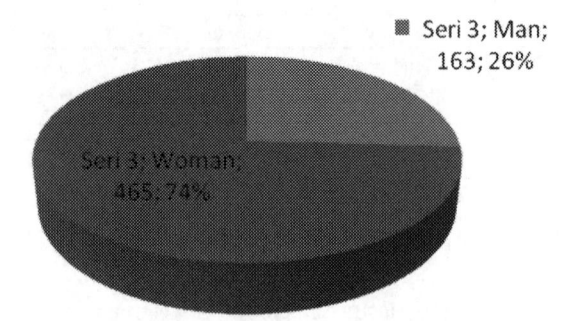

Graph 3.1 Distribution of participants according to gender

Table 3.2 Distribution of participants according to educational status

Variable	Options	Frequency	fi%
Educational Status	Primary school	118	18.8
	Secondary school	74	11.8
	High school	360	57.3
	2-Year college	68	10.8
	4-Year university	8	1.3
	Total	628	100

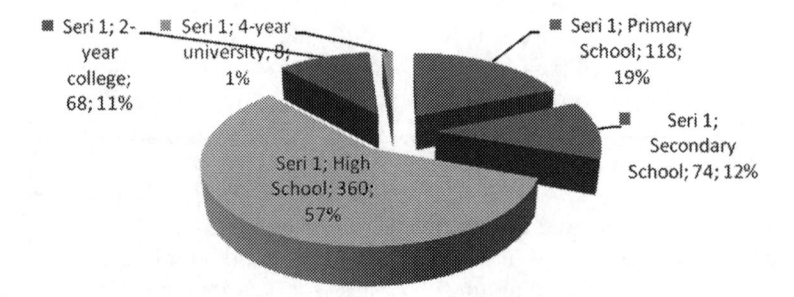

Graph 3.2 Distribution of participants according to educational status

Table 3.3 Distribution of participants according to their marital status

Variable	Options	Frequency	fi%
Marital Status	Married	524	83.4
	Single	104	16.6
	Total	628	100

an income range of 3,701–5,200 TL and 0.2 % had an income range of 5,201 and above. As a result, it can be stated that majority of the employees had a monthly income range of 701–2,200 TL.

Distribution of the employees who participated in the study according to their number of children is presented in Table 3.7 and Graph 3.7. As indicated in the

Graph 3.3 Distribution of participants according to their marital status

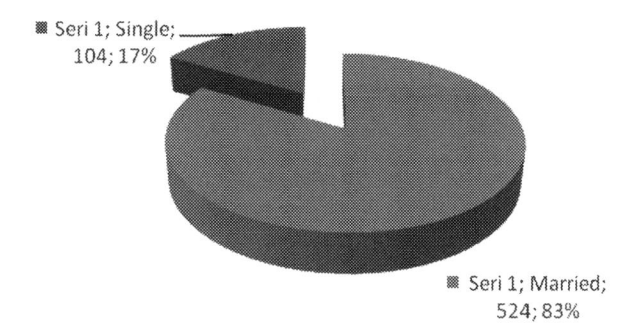

Table 3.4 Distribution of participants according to age groups

Variable	Options	Frequency	fi%
Age	20–30	196	31.2
	31–40	301	47.9
	41–50	128	20.4
	51 and +	3	0.5
	Total	628	100

Graph 3.4 Distribution of participants according to age groups

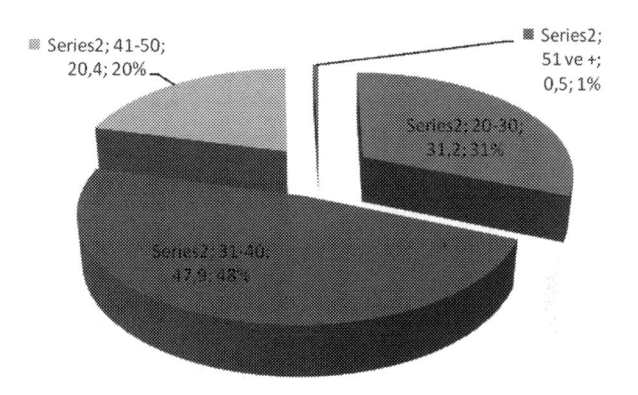

Table 3.5 Distribution of participants according to seniority levels

Variable	Options	Frequency	fi%
Seniority	1–10	335	53.3
	11–20	233	37.1
	21–30	58	9.2
	31 and +	2	0.3
	Total	628	100

table, of the employees, 42.4 % had 1 child; 29.8 % had 2 children; 2.4 % had 3 children; 0.2 % had 4 and more children and 18.6 % had no children.

Distribution of the employees according to the working status of their spouses is presented in Table 3.8 and Graph 3.8. It is understood from the table that 46 % of the spouses of the employees were not working; while 36.5 % of the spouses were working.

Graph 3.5 Distribution of participants according to seniority levels

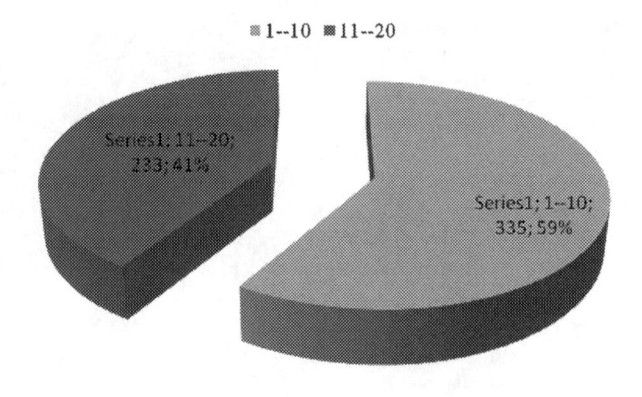

Table 3.6 Distribution of participants according to income levels

Variable	Options	Frequency	fi%
Income status	700 and lower	56	8.9
	701–2,200	544	86.6
	2,201–3,700	23	3.7
	3,701–5,200	4	0.6
	5,201 and +	1	0.2
	Total	628	100

Graph 3.6 Distribution of participants according to income levels

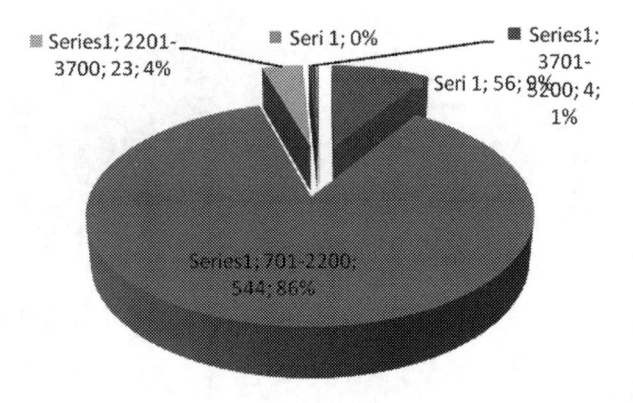

Table 3.7 Distribution of participants according to number of children

Variable	Options	Frequency	fi%
Number of children	1	266	42.4
	2	187	29.8
	3	15	2.4
	4 and above	1	0.2
	None	117	18.6
	Missing system	42	6.7
	Total	628	100

Graph 3.7 Distribution of participants according to number of children

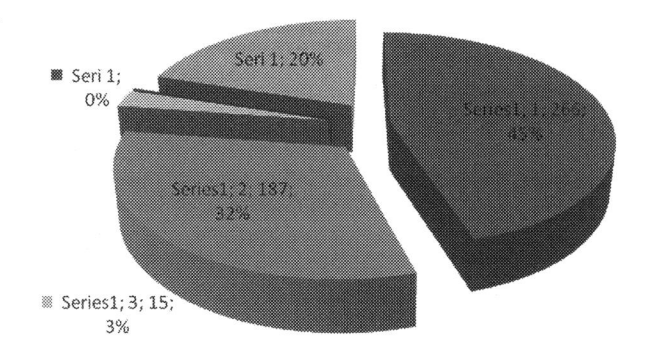

Table 3.8 Distribution of participants according to working status of spouses

Variable	Options	Frequency	fi%
Employment status of spouse	Working	229	36.5
	Not working	289	46.0
	Total	518	82.5
	Missing system	110	17.5
	Total	628	100

Graph 3.8 Distribution of participants according to working status of spouses

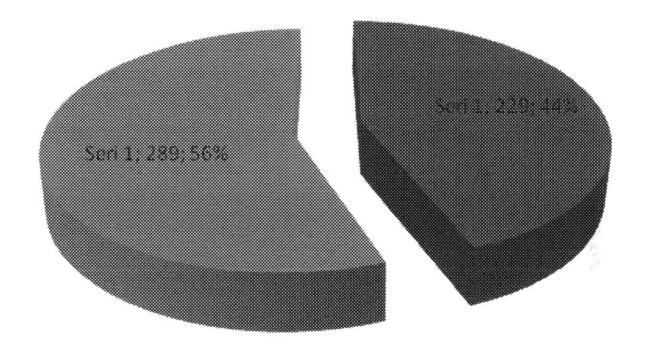

Table 3.9 Distribution of participants according to place of upbringing

Variable	Options	Frequency	fi%
Place of upbringing	Village	247	39.3
	Town	35	5.6
	District	119	18.9
	City	204	32.5
	Large City	23	3.7
	Total	628	100

Distribution of the employees who participated in the study according to their places of upbringing is presented in Table 3.9 and Graph 3.9. As we understood from the table, 39.3 % of the employees were brought up in a village; 5.6 % were brought up in a town; 18.9 % were brought up in a district; 32.5 % were brought up

Graph 3.9 Distribution of participants according to place of upbringing

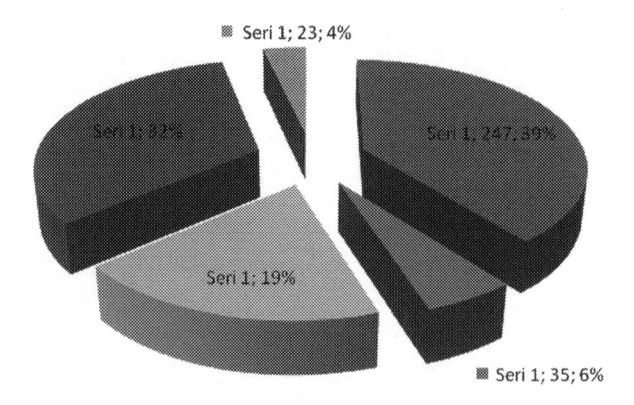

Table 3.10 Distribution of Participants according to Number of Siblings

Variable	Options	Frequency	fi%
Number of siblings	1	16	2.5
	2	239	38.1
	3	171	27.2
	4	109	17.4
	5	37	5.9
	6	33	5.3
	7	11	1.8
	8	11	1.8
	10	1	.2
	Total	628	100

Table 3.11 Distribution of participants according to educational status of fathers

Variable	Options	Frequency	Fi%
Educational status of father	Illiterate	27	4.3
	Primary school	467	74.4
	Secondary school	57	9.1
	High school	62	9.9
	University	15	2.4
	Total	628	100

in a city; 3.7 % were brought up in a large city. It is understood from the table that the majority of the employees were brought up in cities or villages.

Distribution of the participants according to number of siblings is presented in Table 3.10. It is understood from the table that of the employees, 2.5 % had 1 sibling; 38.1 % had 2 siblings; 27.2 % had 3 siblings; 17.4 % had 4 siblings; 5.9 % had 5 siblings; 5.3 % had 6 siblings; 1.8 % had 7 siblings; 1.8 % had 8 siblings; 0.2 % had 10 siblings. Based on these results, it can be stated that majority of the employees had 2 siblings.

Table 3.11 and Graph 3.10 present distribution of participants according to educational status of fathers. It is indicated in the table that of the employees,

Graph 3.10 Distribution of participants according to educational status of fathers

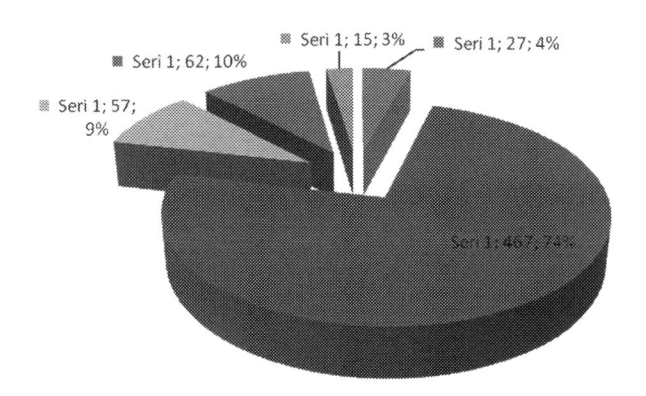

Table 3.12 Distribution of participants according to education status of mother

Variable	Options	Frequency	Fi%
Educational status of mother	Illiterate	81	12.9
	Primary school	452	72.0
	Secondary school	54	8.6
	High school	39	6.2
	University	2	0.3
	Total	628	100

Graph 3.11 Distribution of participants according to education status of mother

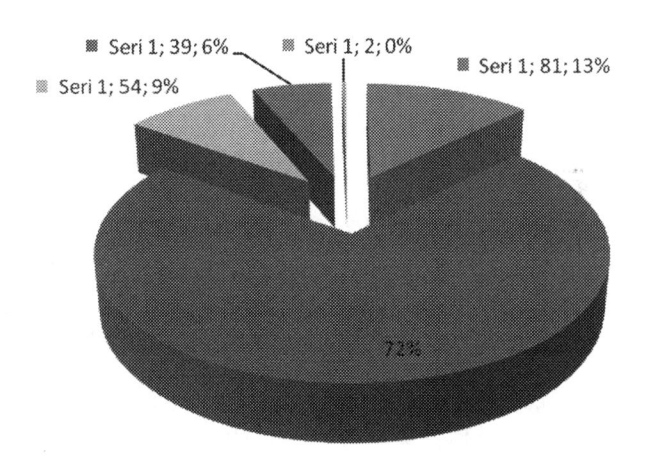

fathers of 4.3 % were illiterate; 74.4 % were primary school graduates; 9.1 % were secondary school graduates; 2.4 % were university graduates. Based on these findings, it can be stated that fathers of the majority of the participants were primary school graduates.

Distribution of the participants according to educational status of mothers is presented in Table 3.12 and Graph 3.11. As we understood from the table, mothers of 12.9 % of the employees were illiterate; 72 % were primary school graduates; 8.6 % were secondary school graduates; 6.2 % were high school graduates and

Table 3.13 Distribution of participants according to sectors

Variable	Options	Frequency	Fi%
Distribution of sectors	Glass	225	40.6
	Textile	221	35.2
	Apparel	152	24.2
	Total	628	100

Graph 3.12 Distribution of participants according to sectors

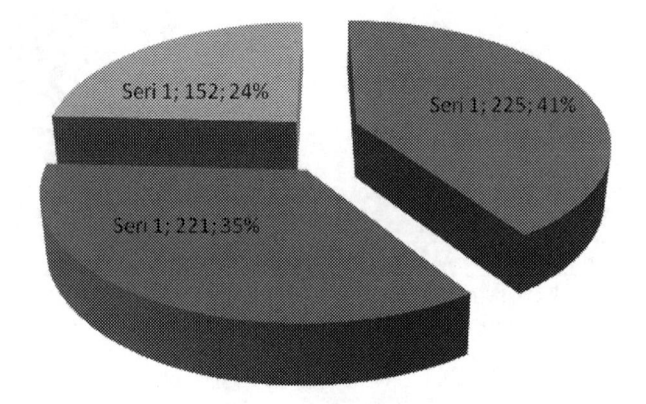

0.3 % were university graduates. Based on these findings, it can be stated that mothers of the majority of the participants were primary school graduates.

Table 3.13 and Graph 3.12 present distribution of the participants according to sectors. As it is understood from the table, 40.6 % of the participants were working in glass sector; 35.2 % were working in textile sector and 24.2 % were working in apparel sector.

3.8   Frequency and Percentage Distributions of Responds to Leadership Behaviour Questionnaire

Frequency, percentage distribution, mean and standard deviations of the responds of the employees to the statements in leadership behavior questionnaire are presented below.

Numerical distribution of the responds of the employees to the statement "Behaviors or my manager are friendly" is presented in Table 3.14. It was found that, of the employees, 6.1 % strongly disagreed; 13.1 % disagreed; 12.9 % were undecided; 38.4 % agreed; 29.6 % strongly agreed with the statement **"Behaviors of my manager are friendly."** Based on these findings, it was found that the majority of the employees agreed with statement 1 and that their managers had friendly behaviors.

Table 3.14 Distribution of the responds of the participants to the statement "Behaviors of my manager are friendly"

1.	Statement	Frequency	Percentage	Mean	Standard deviation
	Strongly disagree	38	6.1		
	Disagree	82	13.1		
	Undecided	81	12.9	3.72	1.191
	Agree	241	38.4		
	Strongly agree	186	29.6		
	Total	628	100.0		

Table 3.15 Distribution of the responds of the participants to the statement "My manager listens to ideas and suggestions of his/her subordinates"

2.	Statement	Frequency	Percentage	Mean	Standard deviation
	Strongly disagree	31	4.9		
	Disagree	78	12.4		
	Undecided	75	11.9	3.76	1.131
	Agree	271	43.2		
	Strongly agree	173	27.5		
	Total	628	100.0		

Table 3.16 Distribution of the responds of the participants to the statement "My manager maintains order at the workplace"

3.	Statement	Frequency	Percentage	Mean	Standard deviation
	Strongly disagree	19	3.0		
	Disagree	51	8.1		
	Undecided	82	13.1	3.93	1.020
	Agree	278	44.3		
	Strongly agree	198	31.5		
	Total	628	100.0		

Table 3.15 shows the numerical distribution of the responds the employees gave to the statement "My manager listens to the ideas and suggestions of his/her subordinates." It was found that of the employees, 4.9 % strongly disagreed; 12.4 % disagreed; 11.9 % were undecided; 43.2 % agreed; 27.5 % strongly agreed with the statement **"My manager listens to the ideas and suggestions of his/her subordinates."** As a result, it was found that majority of the employees agreed with statement 2 and it was found that their managers gave importance and listened to the ideas and suggestions of their subordinates. This result can be considered to increase self-confidence of the subordinates.

Numerical distribution of the responds of the employees to the statement "My manager maintains order at the workplace" is presented in Table 3.16. It was found that of the employees, 3 % strongly disagreed; 8.1 % disagreed; 13.1 were undecided; 44.3 % agreed; 31.5 % strongly agreed with the statement **"My**

Table 3.17 Distribution of the responds of the participants to the statement "My manager trusts to his/her subordinates"

4.	Statement	Frequency	Percentage	Mean	Standard deviation
	Strongly disagree	28	4.5		
	Disagree	64	10.2		
	Undecided	112	17.8	3.78	1.111
	Agree	239	38.1		
	Strongly agree	185	29.5		
	Total	628	100.0		

Table 3.18 Distribution of the responds of the participants to the statement "My manager does not avoid taking risks while making decisions"

5.	Statement	Frequency	Percentage	Mean	Standard deviation
	Strongly disagree	36	5.7		
	Disagree	93	14.8		
	Undecided	131	20.9	3.55	1.157
	Agree	227	36.1		
	Strongly agree	141	22.5		
	Total	628	100.0		

manager maintains order at the workplace". Based on this finding, it was found that majority of the employees agreed with statement 3 and that their managers maintained order at the workplace.

Distribution of the responds of the employees to the statement "My manager trusts to his/her subordinates" is presented in Table 3.17. It was found that, of the participants, 4.5 % strongly disagreed; 10.2 % disagreed; 17.8 % were undecided; 38.1 % agreed; 29.5 % strongly agreed with the statement **"My manager trusts his/her subordinates".** Based on these findings, it was found that majority of the employees agreed with statement 4 and that their managers trusted to their subordinates. The fact that managers trust to subordinates can be considered as a result of positive behavior and successful performance of the subordinates.

Numerical distribution of the responds of the employees to the statement "My manager does not avoid taking risks while making decisions" is presented in Table 3.18. It was found that, of the participants, 5.7 % strongly disagreed; 14.8 % disagreed; 20.9 % were undecided; 36.1 % agreed; 22.5 % strongly agreed with the statement **"My manager does not avoid taking risks while making decisions".** Based on these findings, it was found that majority of employees agreed with statement 5 and that their managers did not avoid taking risks while making decisions. Considering the essence of being a manager is to make decision, it can be stated that the managers who want to be successful do not avoid taking risks.

Table 3.19 shows the distribution of the responds of the employees to the statement "My manager always knows who is responsible for what". It was found that, of the participants, 3.2 % strongly disagreed; 9.4 % disagreed; 12.3 % were

Table 3.19 Distribution of the responds of the participants to the statement "My manager always knows who is responsible for what"

6.	Statement	Frequency	Percentage	Mean	Standard deviation
	Strongly disagree	20	3.2		
	Disagree	59	9.4		
	Undecided	77	12.3	3.90	1.041
	Agree	279	44.4		
	Strongly agree	193	30.7		
	Total	628	100.0		

Table 3.20 Distribution of the responds of the participants to the statement "My manager has open and honest management"

7.	Statement	Frequency	Percentage	Mean	Standard deviation
	Strongly disagree	36	5.7		
	Disagree	75	11.9		
	Undecided	118	18.8	3.68	1.166
	Agree	224	35.7		
	Strongly agree	175	27.9		
	Total	628	100.0		

undecided; 44.4 % agreed; 30.7 % strongly agreed with the statement **"My manager always knows who is responsible for what"**. Based on these findings, it was found that majority of the employees agreed with statement 6 and that their managers knew who is responsible for what. This result shows that the managers have a good communication with their subordinates and that they know their potential.

Table 3.20 shows numerical distribution of the responds of the employees to the statement "My manager always has an open and honest management". It was found that, of the employees, 5.7 % strongly disagreed; 11.9 % disagreed; 18.8 % were undecided; 35.7 % disagreed; 27.9 % strongly agreed with the statement **"My manager always has open and honest management"**. It was found that majority of the employees agreed with statement 7 and that their managers had open and honest management. This result points out to transparent management.

Numerical distribution of the responds of the employees to the statement "My manager encourages new ideas" is presented in Table 3.21. It was found that, of the participants, 5.4 % strongly disagreed; 12.3 % disagreed; 17.8 % were undecided; 38.4 % agreed and 26.1 % strongly agreed with the statement **"My manager encourages new ideas"**. Based on these findings, it can be stated that majority of the employees agreed with statement 8 and that their managers encouraged new ideas. It can be stated that subordinates make attempt to produce new ideas. On the other hand, it can be thought that people who produce new ideas are motivated by various rewards and that the employees who see that new ideas are rewarded will be motivated to produce more new ideas.

Table 3.21 Distribution of the responds of the participants to the statement "My manager always encourages new ideas"

8.	Statement	Frequency	Percentage	Mean	Standard deviation
	Strongly disagree	34	5.4		
	Disagree	77	12.3		
	Undecided	112	17.8	3.68	1.146
	Agree	241	38.4		
	Strongly agree	164	26.1		
	Total	628	100.0		

Table 3.22 Distribution of the responds of the participants to the statement "My manager has consistent behaviors"

9.	Statement	Frequency	Percentage	Mean	Standard deviation
	Strongly disagree	31	4.9		
	Disagree	87	13.9		
	Undecided	93	14.8	3.70	1.152
	Agree	247	39.3		
	Strongly agree	170	27.1		
	Total	628	100.0		

Table 3.23 Distribution of the responds of the participants to the statement "My manager is open to criticism"

10	Statement	Frequency	Percentage	Mean	Standard deviation
	Strongly disagree	44	7.0		
	Disagree	106	16.9		
	Undecided	108	17.2	3.53	1.227
	Agree	214	34.1		
	Strongly agree	156	24.8		
	Total	628	100.0		

Table 3.22 shows numerical distribution of the responds of the employees to the statement "My manager has consistent behaviors". It was found that of the employees, 4.9 % strongly disagreed; 13.9 % disagreed; 14.8 % were undecided; 39.3 % agreed and 27.1 % strongly agreed with the statement **"My manager has consistent behaviors"**. Based on these findings it was found that majority of the employees agreed with statement 9 and that their managers had consistent behaviors. It can be stated that a manager who wants to be respected should show consistency in his/her behaviors.

Table 3.23 presents numerical distribution of the responds of the employees to the statement "My manager is open to criticism". It was found that of the employees, 7 % strongly disagreed; 16.9 % disagreed; 17.2 % were undecided; 34.1 % agreed; 24.8 % strongly agreed with the statement **"My manager is open to criticism"**. Based on these findings, it was found that majority of the employees agreed with statement 10 and that their managers were open to criticism. This result

Table 3.24 Distribution of the responds of the participants to the statement "My manager likes discussing new ideas"

11.	Statement	Frequency	Percentage	Mean	Standard deviation
	Strongly disagree	43	6.8		
	Disagree	85	13.5		
	Undecided	131	20.9	3.55	1.183
	Agree	222	35.4		
	Strongly agree	147	23.4		
	Total	628	100.0		

Table 3.25 Distribution of the responds of the participants to the statement "My manager gives importance to obeying the rules and principles"

12.	Statement	Frequency	Percentage	Mean	Standard deviation
	Strongly disagree	20	3.2		
	Disagree	43	6.8		
	Undecided	54	8.6	4.01	0.988
	Agree	305	48.6		
	Strongly agree	206	32.8		
	Total	628	100.0		

indicates that the managers establish a good communication with their subordinates and that they consider criticism towards them as an opportunity for development.

Table 3.24 indicates numerical distribution of the responds of employees to the statement "My manager likes discussing new ideas". It was found that, of the employees, 6.8 % strongly disagreed; 13.5 % disagreed; 20.9 % were undecided; 35.4 % agreed; 23.4 % strongly disagreed with the statement **"My manager likes discussing new ideas"**. As a result, it was found that majority of the employees agreed with statement 11 and that their managers liked discussing new ideas. Considering that discussing various ideas will significantly contribute to solution of problems, it can be stated that this result will be beneficial for the enterprises.

Numerical distribution of the responds of the employees to the statement "My manager gives importance to obeying rules and principles" is presented in Table 3.25. It was found that, of the participants, 3.2 % strongly disagreed; 6.8 % disagreed; 8.6 % were undecided; 48.6 % agreed; 32.8 % strongly agreed with the statement **"My manager gives importance to obeying rules and principles"**. Based on these findings, it was found that majority of the participants agreed with statement 12 and their managers gave importance to obeying rules and principles. This result shows that the managers obey the norms in their enterprises. It can be stated that subordinates who observed that their managers obey the norms will show much more respect to norms and they will adopt these norms.

Table 3.26 presents numerical distribution of the responds of the employees to the statement "My manager inspires trust". Of the employees, 6.1 % strongly disagreed; 11.8 % disagreed; 17.8 % were undecided; 37.4 % agreed; 26.9 % strongly agreed with the statement **"My manager inspires trust"**. Based on

Table 3.26 Distribution of the responds of the participants to the statement "My manager inspires trust"

13.	Statement	Frequency	Percentage	Mean	Standard deviation
	Strongly disagree	38	6.1		
	Disagree	74	11.8		
	Undecided	112	17.8	3.67	1.166
	Agree	235	37.4		
	Strongly agree	169	26.9		
	Total	628	100.0		

Table 3.27 Distribution of the responds of the participants to the statement "My manager makes plans for the future"

14.	Statement	Frequency	Percentage	Mean	Standard deviation
	Strongly disagree	30	4.8		
	Disagree	71	11.3		
	Undecided	141	22.5	3.67	1.122
	Agree	222	35.4		
	Strongly agree	164	26.1		
	Total	628	100.0		

Table 3.28 Distribution of the responds of the participants to the statement "My manager gives information about the results of the units"

15.	Statement	Frequency	Percentage	Mean	Standard deviation
	Strongly disagree	51	8.1		
	Disagree	100	15.9		
	Undecided	112	17.8	3.49	1.230
	Agree	222	35.4		
	Strongly agree	143	22.8		
	Total	628	100.0		

these findings, it was found that majority of employees agreed with statement 13 and that their managers inspired confidence. This result reveals that the managers in the enterprises included in the study gained the trust of their subordinates by their behaviors and applications.

Table 3.27 presents numerical distribution of the responds of the employees to the statement "My manager makes plans for the future". It was found that 4.8 % of the participants strongly disagreed; 11.3 % disagreed; 22.5 % were undecided; 35.4 % agreed and 26.1 % strongly disagreed with the statement **"My manager makes plans for the future"**. Based on these findings, it was found that majority of the employees agreed with statement 14 and that their managers made plans for the future. This result reveals that the managers gave importance to planning and that they were had vision.

Table 3.28 shows numerical distribution of the responds of the employees to the statement "My manager gives information about the results of the units". It was

Table 3.29 Distribution of the responds of the participants to the statement "My manager appreciates good work"

16	Statement	Frequency	Percentage	Mean	Standard deviation
	Strongly disagree	49	7.8		
	Disagree	83	13.2		
	Undecided	92	14.6	3.65	1.249
	Agree	216	34.4		
	Strongly agree	188	29.9		
	Total	628	100.0		

Table 3.30 Distribution of the responds of the participants to the statement "My manager encourages growth"

17.	Statement	Frequency	Percentage	Mean	Standard deviation
	Strongly disagree	24	3.8		
	Disagree	74	11.8		
	Undecided	107	17.0	3.76	1.100
	Agree	247	39.3		
	Strongly agree	176	28.0		
	Total	628	100.0		

found that, of the employees, 8.1 % strongly disagreed; 15.9 % disagreed; 17.8 % were undecided; 35.4 % agreed; 22.8 % strongly agreed with the statement **"My manager gives information about the results of the units"**. Based on these results, it was found that majority of the employees agreed with statement 15 and that their managers gave information about the results of the units. The subordinates who receive feedback can correct their mistakes and reinforce positive behaviors.

Table 3.29 shows the distribution of the responds of the participants to the statement "My manager appreciates good work". It was found that, of the participants, 7.8 % strongly disagreed; 13.2 % disagreed; 14.6 % were undecided; 34.4 % agreed; 29.9 % strongly agreed with the statement **"My manager appreciates good work"**. Based on these findings it was found that majority of the employees agreed with statement 16 and that their managers appreciated good work. This result shows that the managers established good communication and dialogue with their employees. On the other hand, it can be stated that the subordinates whose good work is appreciated by their managers will be honored and motivated.

Table 3.30 indicated numerical distribution of the responds of the employees to the statement "My manager encourages growth". It was found that, of the participants, 3.8 % strongly disagreed; 11.8 % disagreed; 17 % were undecided; 39.3 % agreed; 28 % strongly agreed with the statement **"My manager encourages growth"**. Based on this finding it can be stated that majority of the employees agreed with statement 17 and that their managers encouraged growth.

Table 3.31 presents numerical distribution of the responds of the employees to the statement "My manager sets clear objectives". It was found that, of the employees, 4 % strongly disagreed; 10.5 % disagreed; 17.8 % were undecided;

Table 3.31 Distribution of the responds of the participants to the statement "My manager sets clear objectives"

18.	Statement	Frequency	Percentage	Mean	Standard deviation
	Strongly disagree	25	4.0		
	Disagree	66	10.5		
	Undecided	112	17.8	3.75	1.089
	Agree	258	41.1		
	Total	166	26.4		
		628	100.0		

Table 3.32 Distribution of the responds of the participants to the statement "My manager gives importance to the opinions of his/her subordinates"

19.	Statement	Frequency	Percentage	Mean	Standard deviation
	Strongly disagree	44	7.0		
	Disagree	75	11.9		
	Undecided	128	20.4	3.60	1.184
	Agree	224	35.7		
	Strongly agree	157	25.0		
	Total	628	100.0		

41.1 % agreed; 26.4 % strongly agreed with the statement **"My manager sets clear objectives"**. Based on these findings, it can be stated that majority of the employees agreed with the statement 18 and that their managers set clear objectives and did not leave their work to chance.

Numerical distribution of the responds of the employees to the statement "My manager gives importance to the opinions of his/her subordinates" is presented in Table 3.32. It was found that, of the employees, 7 % strongly disagreed; 11.9 % disagreed; 20.4 % were undecided; 35.7 % agreed; 25 % strongly agreed with the statement **"My manager gives importance to the opinions of his/her subordinates"**. Based on these results it was found that majority of the employees agreed with statement 19 and that their managers gave importance to opinions of their subordinates. This result can suggest that managers give importance and value the opinions of their subordinates.

Table 3.33 presents numerical distribution of the responds of the employees to the statement "My manager produces new projects". It was found that of the participants, 5.1 % strongly disagreed; 11 % disagreed; 18.8 % were undecided; 39.8 % agreed; 25.3 % strongly agreed with the statement **"My manager produces new projects"**. Based on these findings, it was found that the majority of the employees agreed with statement 20 and that their managers produced new projects. In other words, it can be stated that the managers are open to change and development.

Table 3.34 represents numerical distribution of the responds of the employees to the statement "My manager is very meticulous on the implemented plans". It was found that, of the employees, 4 % strongly disagreed; 9.2 % disagreed; 16 % were

Table 3.33 Distribution of the responds of the participants to the statement "My manager produces new projects"

20.	Statement	Frequency	Percentage	Mean	Standard deviation
	Strongly disagree	32	5.1		
	Disagree	69	11.0		
	Undecided	118	18.8	3.69	1.117
	Agree	250	39.8		
	Strongly agree	159	25.3		
	Total	628	100.0		

Table 3.34 Distribution of the responds of the participants to the statement "My manager is very meticulous on the implemented plans"

21.	Statement	Frequency	Percentage	Mean	Standard deviation
	Strongly disagree	25	4.0		
	Disagree	58	9.2		
	Undecided	100	16.0	3.83	1.071
	Agree	264	42.0		
	Strongly agree	181	28.8		
	Total	628	100.0		

Table 3.35 Distribution of the responds of the participants to the statement "My manager defends his/her subordinates"

22.	Statement	Frequency	Percentage	Mean	Standard deviation
	Strongly disagree	50	8.0		
	Disagree	91	14.5		
	Undecided	117	18.6	3.53	1.227
	Agree	217	34.6		
	Strongly agree	153	24.4		
	Total	628	100.0		

undecided; 42.1 % agreed; 28.9 % strongly agreed with the statement **"My manager is very meticulous on the implemented plans"**. Based on these findings, it was found that the majority of the employees agreed with statement 21 and that their managers behaved meticulously on the implemented plans. In other words, it can be stated that the managers are sensitive in practice.

Table 3.35 presents the responds of the employees to the statement "My manager defends his/her subordinates". It was found that, of the employees, 8 % strongly disagreed; 14.5 % disagreed; 18.6 % were undecided; 34.6 % agreed; 24.4 % strongly agreed with the statement **"My manager defends his/her subordinates"**. Based on these findings, it was found that the majority of the employees agreed with statement 22 and that their managers defended their subordinates. In other words, it can be stated that the managers protect the rights of their subordinates against their colleagues or other managers.

Table 3.36 Distribution of the responds of the participants to the statement "My manager is open to innovation"

23.	Statement	Frequency	Percentage	Mean	Standard deviation
	Strongly disagree	27	4.3		
	Disagree	72	11.5		
	Undecided	117	18.6	3.72	1.103
	Agree	247	39.3		
	Strongly agree	165	26.3		
	Total	628	100.0		

Table 3.37 Distribution of the responds of the participants to the statement "My manager is meticulous in inspection of the work"

24.	Statement	Frequency	Percentage	Mean	Standard deviation
	Strongly disagree	12	1.9		
	Disagree	49	7.8		
	Undecided	64	10.2	4.04	0.969
	Agree	281	44.7		
	Strongly agree	222	35.4		
	Total	628	100.0		

Table 3.36 presents the numerical distribution of the responds of the employees to the statement "My manager is open to innovation". It was found that, of the participants, 4.3 % strongly disagreed; 11.5 % disagreed; 18.6 % were undecided; 39.3 % agreed; 26.3 % strongly agreed with the statement "**My manager is open to innovation**". Based on these findings, it was found that the majority of the employees agreed with statement 23 and that their managers were open to innovation. This result shows that managers are open to innovation in their enterprises.

Table 3.37 presents the numerical distribution of the responds of employees to the statement "My manager is meticulous in inspection of the work". It was found that, of the employees, 1.9 % strongly disagreed; 7.8 % disagreed; 10.2 % were undecided; 44.7 % agreed; 35.4 % strongly agreed with the statement "**My manager is meticulous in inspection of the work**". Based on these findings, it was found that the majority of the employees agreed with statement 24 and that their managers were meticulous in inspection of work.

Table 3.38 presents numerical distribution of the responds of the employees to the statement "My manager creates a friendly environment without dispute". It was found that, of the employees, 8 % strongly disagreed; 16.7 % disagreed; 16.9 % were undecided; 34.2 % agreed; 24.2 % strongly agreed with the statement "**My manager creates a friendly environment without dispute**". Based on these findings, it was found that the majority of the employees agreed with statement 25 and that their managers created a friendly environment without any disputes in the workplace.

Table 3.39 presents numerical distribution of the responds of the employees to the statement "My manager creates opportunities to eliminate conflicts". It was

Table 3.38 Distribution of the responds of the participants to the statement "My manager creates a friendly environment without disputes"

25.	Statement	Frequency	Percentage	Mean	Standard deviation
	Strongly disagree	50	8.0		
	Disagree	105	16.7		
	Undecided	106	16.9	3.50	1.244
	Agree	215	34.2		
	Strongly agree	152	24.2		
	Total	628	100.0		

Table 3.39 Distribution of the responds of the participants to the statement "My manager creates opportunities to eliminate conflicts"

26.	Statement	Frequency	Percentage	Mean	Standard deviation
	Strongly disagree	40	6.4		
	Disagree	82	13.1		
	Undecided	110	17.5	3.62	1.170
	Agree	243	38.7		
	Strongly agree	153	24.4		
	Total	628	100.0		

Table 3.40 Distribution of the responds of the participants to the statement "My manager clearly defines and expresses working requirements"

27.	Statement	Frequency	Percentage	Mean	Standard deviation
	Strongly disagree	25	4.0		
	Disagree	74	11.8		
	Undecided	94	15.0	3.75	1.080
	Agree	278	44.3		
	Strongly agree	157	25.0		
	Total	628	100.0		

found that, of the employees, 6.4 % strongly disagreed; 13.1 % disagreed; 17.5 % were undecided; 38.7 % agreed; 24.4 % strongly agreed with the statement "**My manager creates opportunities to eliminate conflicts**". Based on these findings, it was found that the majority of the employees agreed with statement 26 and that their managers created opportunities to eliminate conflicts. In other words, it can be stated that the managers are successful in solving conflicts.

Table 3.40 presents numerical distribution of the responds of the employees to the statement "My manager clearly defines and expresses working requirements". It was found that, of the employees, 4 % strongly disagreed; 11.8 % disagreed; 15 % were undecided; 44.3 % agreed; 25 % strongly agreed with the statement "**My manager clearly defines and expresses working requirements**". Based on these findings, it was found that the majority of the employees agreed with statement

Table 3.41 Distribution of the responds of the participants to the statement "My manager treats his/her subordinates fairly"

28.	Statement	Frequency	Percentage	Mean	Standard deviation
	Strongly disagree	51	8.1		
	Disagree	97	15.4		
	Undecided	120	19.1	3.49	1.241
	Agree	212	33.8		
	Strongly agree	148	23.6		
	Total	628	100.0		

Table 3.42 Distribution of the responds of the participants to the statement "My manager makes quick decisions when required"

29.	Statement	Frequency	Percentage	Mean	Standard deviation
	Strongly disagree	20	3.2		
	Disagree	57	9.1		
	Undecided	93	14.8	3.84	1.022
	Agree	289	46.0		
	Strongly agree	169	26.9		
	Total	628	100.0		

27 and that their managers clearly defined and expressed working requirements. In other words, it can be stated that the managers made good work definition.

Table 3.41 indicates numerical distribution of the responds of the employees to the statement "My manager treats his/her subordinates fairly". It was found that, of the employees, 8.1 % strongly disagreed; 15.4 % disagreed; 19.1 % were undecided; 33.8 % agreed; 23.6 % strongly agreed with the statement **"My manager treats his/her subordinates fairly"**. Based on these results, it was found that the majority of the employees agreed with the statement 28 and that their managers treated their subordinates fairly. It can be stated that the managers treat their subordinates equally.

Table 3.42 indicates numerical distribution of the responds of the employees to the statement "My manager makes quick decisions when required". It was found that, of the employees, 3.2 % strongly disagreed; 9.1 % disagreed; 14.8 % were undecided; 46 % agreed; 26.9 % strongly agreed with the statement **"My manager makes quick decisions when required"**. Based on these findings, it was found that the majority of the employees agreed with statement 29 and that their managers made quick decisions when required.

Table 3.43 indicates numerical distribution of the responds of the participants to the statement "My manager makes plans carefully". It was found that, of the employees, 3.5 % strongly disagreed; 9.1 % disagreed; 18.3 % were undecided; 41.4 % agreed; 27.7 % strongly agreed with the statement **"My manager makes plans carefully"**. It was found that, the majority of the employees agreed with statement 30 and that their managers made plans carefully.

Table 3.43 Distribution of the responds of the participants to the statement "My manager makes plans carefully"

30.	Statement	Frequency	Percentage	Mean	Standard deviation
	Strongly disagree	22	3.5		
	Disagree	57	9.1		
	Undecided	115	18.3	3.81	1.050
	Agree	260	41.4		
	Strongly agree	174	27.7		
	Total	628	100.0		

Table 3.44 Distribution of the responds of the participants to the statement "My manager gives his/her subordinates the right to speak while making decisions"

31.	Statement	Frequency	Percentage	Mean	Standard deviation
	Strongly disagree	52	8.3		
	Disagree	99	15.8		
	Undecided	110	17.5	3.51	1.248
	Agree	212	33.8		
	Strongly agree	155	24.7		
	Total	628	100.0		

Table 3.45 Distribution of the responds of the participants to the statement "My manager is flexible and open to change"

32.	Statement	Frequency	Percentage	Mean	Standard deviation
	Strongly disagree	40	6.4		
	Disagree	79	12.6		
	Undecided	119	18.9	3.62	1.170
	Agree	234	37.3		
	Strongly agree	156	24.8		
	Total	628	100.0		

Table 3.44 presents numerical distribution of the responds of the employees to the statement "My manager gives his/her subordinates the right to speak while making decisions". It was found that, of the employees, 8.3 % strongly disagreed; 15.8 % disagreed; 17.5 % were undecided; 33.8 % agreed; 24.7 % strongly agreed with the statement **"My manager gives his/her subordinates the right to speak while making decisions"**. It was found that the majority of the employees agreed with statement 31 and that their managers gave their subordinates the right to speak and they valued their opinions.

Table 3.45 indicates numerical distribution of the responds of the employees to the statement **"My manager is flexible and open to change"**. It was found that, of the employees, 6.4 % strongly disagreed; 12.6 % disagreed; 18.9 % were undecided; 37.3 % agreed; 24.8 % strongly agreed with statement 32. As a result, it was found that the majority of the employees agreed with this statement and that their managers were flexible and open to criticism.

Table 3.46 Distribution of the responds of the participants to the statement "My manager gives clear instructions"

33.	Statement	Frequency	Percentage	Mean	Standard deviation
	Strongly disagree	17	2.7		
	Disagree	60	9.6		
	Undecided	58	9.2	3.95	1.018
	Agree	293	46.7		
	Strongly agree	200	31.8		
	Total	628	100.0		

Table 3.47 Distribution of the responds of the participants to the statement "My manager respects his/her subordinates as individuals"

34.	Statement	Frequency	Percentage	Mean	Standard deviation
	Strongly disagree	41	6.5		
	Disagree	65	10.4		
	Undecided	105	16.7	3.70	1.165
	Agree	245	39.0		
	Strongly agree	172	27.4		
	Total	628	100.0		

Table 3.46 indicates numerical distribution of the responds of the employees to the statement "My manager gives clear instructions". It was found that, of the employees, 2.7 % strongly disagreed; 9.6 % disagreed; 9.2 % were undecided; 46.7 % agreed; 31.8 % strongly agreed with statement **"My manager gives clear instructions"**. It was found that the majority of the employees agreed with statement 33 and that their managers gave clear instructions.

Table 3.47 indicates numerical distribution of the responds of the employees to the statement "My manager respects his/her subordinates as individuals". It was found that, of the employees, 6.5 % strongly disagreed; 10.4 % disagreed; 16.7 % were undecided; 39 % agreed; 27.4 % strongly agreed with the statement **"My manager respects his/her subordinates as individuals"**. It was found that the majority of the employees agreed with statement 34 and that their managers respected their subordinates as individuals.

Table 3.48 indicates numerical distribution of the responds of the employees to the statement "My manager shows new and different ideas to the implementation of works". It was found that, of the employees, 3.8 % strongly disagreed; 9.7 % disagreed; 18.2 % were undecided; 40.8 % agreed; 27.5 % strongly agreed with the statement **"My manager shows new and different ideas to the implementation of works"**. It was found that the majority of the employees agreed with statement 35 and that their managers showed new and different ideas to the implementation of works. In other words, it can be stated that their managers were creative in practice.

Table 3.49 indicates numerical distribution of the responds of the employees to the statement "My manager analyzes situations and does not make decisions

Table 3.48 Distribution of the responds of the participants to the statement "My manager shows new and different ideas to the implementation of works"

35.	Statement	Frequency	Percentage	Mean	Standard deviation
	Strongly disagree	24	3.8		
	Disagree	61	9.7		
	Undecided	114	18.2	3.79	1.070
	Agree	256	40.8		
	Strongly agree	173	27.5		
	Total	628	100.0		

Table 3.49 Distribution of the responds of the participants to the statement "My manager analyzes situations and does not make decisions without thinking"

36.	Statement	Frequency	Percentage	Mean	Standard deviation
	Strongly disagree	36	5.7		
	Disagree	67	10.7		
	Undecided	106	16.9	3.71	1.140
	Agree	251	40.0		
	Strongly agree	168	26.8		
	Total	628	100.0		

without thinking". It was found that, of the employees, 5.7 % strongly disagreed; 10.7 % disagreed; 16.9 % were undecided; 40 % agreed; 26.8 % strongly agreed with the statement **"My manager analyzes situations and does not make decisions without thinking".** It was found that the majority of the employees agreed with statement 36 and that their managers analyzed situations and did not make decisions without thinking.

3.9 Frequency and Percentage Distributions of Responds to Communication Scale Questionnaire

Frequency and percentage distributions of the responds of the employees to the statements in communication scale are presented in this section.

Table 3.50 indicates numerical distribution of the responds of the employees to the statement "My manager motivates the employees using his/her communication skills". It was found that, of the employees, 8 % strongly disagreed; 15.4% disagreed; 17.5 % were undecided; 36.5 % agreed; 22.6 % strongly disagreed with the statement **"My manager motivates the employees using his/her communication skills".** It was found that the majority of the employees agreed with statement 1 and that their managers motivated their employees using their communication skills. Furthermore, it can be stated that the manager value motivation.

Table 3.51 indicates numerical distribution of the responds of the employees to the statement "My manager informs the employees about the results of the work

Table 3.50 Distribution of the responds of the participants to the statement "My manager motivates the employees using his/her communication skills"

1.	Statement	Frequency	Percentage	Mean	Standard deviation
	Strongly disagree	50	8.0		
	Disagree	97	15.4		
	Undecided	110	17.5	3.50	1.221
	Agree	229	36.5		
	Strongly agree	142	22.6		
	Total	628	100.0		

Table 3.51 Distribution of the responds of the participants to the statement "My manager informs the employees about the results of the work they perform"

2.	Statement	Frequency	Percentage	Mean	Standard deviation
	Strongly disagree	38	6.1		
	Disagree	109	17.4		
	Undecided	82	13.1	3.57	1.186
	Agree	258	41.1		
	Strongly agree	141	22.5		
	Total	628	100.0		

Table 3.52 Distribution of the responds of the participants to the statement "My manager holds periodic meeting with the employees to listen to their problems"

3.	Statement	Frequency	Percentage	Mean	Standard deviation
	Strongly disagree	70	11.1		
	Disagree	139	22.1		
	Undecided	74	11.8	3.33	1.340
	Agree	201	32.0		
	Strongly agree	144	22.9		
	Total	628	100.0		

they perform". It was found that, of the participants, 6.1 % strongly disagreed; 17.4 % disagreed; 13.1 % were undecided; 41.1 % agreed; 22.5 % strongly agreed with the statement **"My manager informs the employees about the results of the work they perform"**. It was found that the majority of the participants agreed with statement 2 and that their managers informed their employees about the results of the work they perform. This result indicates that the managers give importance to giving feedback.

Table 3.52 indicates numerical distribution of the responds of the employees to the statement "My manager holds periodic meeting with the employees to listen to their problems." It was found that, of the employees, 6.1 % strongly disagreed; 17.4 % disagreed; 13.1 % were undecided; 41.1 % agreed; 22.5 % strongly agreed with the statement **"My manager holds periodic meeting with the employees to listen to their problems"**. It was found that the majority of the employees agreed

Table 3.53 Distribution of the responds of the participants to the statement "My manager holds meetings with the employees to solve problems"

4.	Statement	Frequency	Percentage	Mean	Standard deviation
	Strongly disagree	67	10.7		
	Disagree	119	18.9		
	Undecided	77	12.3	3.41	1.316
	Agree	218	34.7		
	Strongly agree	147	23.4		
	Total	628	100.0		

Table 3.54 Distribution of the responds of the participants to the statement "My manager uses written communication channels to make sure that his/her employees can understand the orders"

5.	Statement	Frequency	Percentage	Mean	Standard deviation
	Strongly disagree	45	7.2		
	Disagree	114	18.2		
	Undecided	76	12.1	3.53	1.227
	Agree	248	39.5		
	Strongly agree	145	23.1		
	Total	628	100.0		

with statement 3 and that their managers held periodic meetings with the employees to listen to their problems.

Table 3.53 presents numerical distribution of the responds of the employees to the statement "My manager holds meetings with the employees to solve problems". It was found that, of the employees, 10.7 % strongly disagreed; 18.9 % disagreed; 12.3 % were undecided; 34.7 % agreed; 23.4 % strongly agreed with the statement **"My manager holds meetings with the employees to solve problems"**. It was found that the majority of the employees agreed with statement 4 and that their managers held meetings with the employees to solve problems.

Table 3.54 presents numerical distribution of the responds of the employees to the statement "My manager uses written communication channels to make sure that his/her employees can understand the orders". It was found that, of the employees, 7.2 % strongly disagreed; 18.2 % disagreed; 12.1 % were undecided; 39.5 % agreed and 23.1 % strongly agreed with the statement **"My manager uses written communication channels to make sure that his/her employees can understand the orders"**. It was found that the majority of the employees agreed with statement 5 and that their managers used written communication channels to make sure that their employees can understand their orders.

Table 3.55 shows numerical distribution of the responds of the employees to the statement "When the employees have a problem, they can always share this with the manager". It was found that, of the employees, 7.6 % strongly disagreed; 10 % disagreed; 11.1 % were undecided; 42.2 % agreed; 29.1 % strongly agreed with the statement **"When the employees have a problem, they can always share this**

Table 3.55 Distribution of the Responds of the Participants to the statement "When the employees have a problem, they can always share this with the manager"

6.	Statement	Frequency	Percentage	Mean	Standard deviation
	Strongly disagree	48	7.6		
	Disagree	63	10.0		
	Undecided	70	11.1	3.75	1.196
	Agree	265	42.2		
	Strongly agree	182	29.0		
	Total	628	100.0		

Table 3.56 Distribution of the responds of the participants to the statement "My manager establishes relaxed communication with the employees"

7.	Statement	Frequency	Percentage	Mean	Standard deviation
	Strongly disagree	43	6.8		
	Disagree	75	11.9		
	Undecided	80	12.7	3.71	1.192
	Agree	253	40.3		
	Strongly agree	177	28.2		
	Total	628	100.0		

with the manager". It was found that the majority of the employees agreed with statement 6 and that when the employees have a problem, they can always share it with the manager. In other words, it can be stated that the managers adopt and implement an open door policy.

Table 3.56 indicates numerical distribution of the responds of the employees to the statement "My manager establishes relaxed communication with the employees". It was found that, of the students, 6.8 % strongly disagreed; 11.9 % disagreed; 12.7 % were undecided; 40.3 % agreed; 28.2 % strongly agreed with the statement **"My manager establishes relaxed communication with the employees".** Thus, it was found that the majority of the employees agreed with statement 7 and that their managers established relaxed communication with the employees.

Table 3.57 shows numerical distribution of the responds of the employees to the statement "If employees have an idea or suggestion about the work, they share this with their managers". It was found that, of the managers, 5.1 % strongly disagreed; 11.9 % disagreed; 14.5 % were undecided; 41.1 % agreed; 27.4 % strongly agreed with the statement **"If employees have an idea or suggestion about the work, they share this with their managers".** It was found that the majority of the employees agreed with statement 8 and that when the employees had an idea or suggestion about the work, they shared it with their managers. This result shows that the managers encourage their employees to think about the work.

Table 3.58 shows numerical distribution of the responds of the employees to the statement "My manager spares enough time to listen to the employees". It was found that, of the employees, 10.2 % strongly disagreed; 17.4 % disagreed; 13.9 %

Table 3.57 Distribution of the responds of the participants to the statement "If employees have an idea or suggestion about the work, they share this with their managers"

8.	Statement	Frequency	Percentage	Mean	Standard deviation
	Strongly disagree	32	5.1		
	Disagree	75	11.9		
	Undecided	91	14.5	3.74	1.135
	Agree	258	41.1		
	Strongly agree	172	27.4		
	Total	628	100.0		

Table 3.58 Distribution of the responds of the participants to the statement "My manager spares enough time to listen to the employees"

9.	Statement	Frequency	Percentage	Mean	Standard deviation
	Strongly disagree	64	10.2		
	Disagree	109	17.4		
	Undecided	87	13.9	3.44	1.289
	Agree	225	35.8		
	Strongly agree	143	22.8		
	Total	628	100.0		

Table 3.59 Distribution of the responds of the participants to the statement "My manager informs me about the situation in the work place"

10.	Statement	Frequency	Percentage	Mean	Standard deviation
	Strongly disagree	88	14.0		
	Disagree	169	26.9		
	Undecided	100	15.9	3.06	1.336
	Agree	161	25.6		
	Strongly agree	110	17.5		
	Total	628	100.0		

were undecided; 35.8 % agreed; 22.8 % strongly agreed with statement **"My manager spares enough time to listen to the employees"**. It was found that the majority of the employees agreed with statement 9 and that their managers spared enough time to listen to their employees and that they valued them.

Table 3.59 indicates numerical distribution of the responds of the employees to the statement "My manager informs me about the situation in the work place". I was found that, of the employees, 14 % strongly disagreed; 26.9 % disagreed; 15.9 % were undecided; 25.6 % agreed; 17.5 % strongly agreed with the statement **"My manager informs me about the situation in the work place"**. It was found that the majority of the employees agreed with statement 10 and that their managers informed the employees about the situation in the work place and that they gave importance to their employees.

Table 3.60 indicates numerical distribution of the responds of the employees to the statement "My manager congratulates me when I successfully fulfill my task". It

Table 3.60 Distribution of the responds of the participants to the statement "My manager congratulates me when I successfully fulfill my task"

11.	Statement	Frequency	Percentage	Mean	Standard deviation
	Strongly disagree	73	11.6		
	Disagree	114	18.2		
	Undecided	95	15.1	3.35	1.309
	Agree	213	33.9		
	Strongly agree	133	21.2		
	Total	628	100.0		

Table 3.61 Distribution of the responds of the participants to the statement "My manager fully informs the employees about the work they will perform to make them successful in that work"

12.	Statement	Frequency	Percentage	Mean	Standard deviation
	Strongly disagree	48	7.6		
	Disagree	107	17.0		
	Undecided	97	15.4	3.52	1.240
	Agree	223	35.5		
	Strongly agree	153	24.4		
	Total	628	100.0		

was found that, of the employees, 11.6 % strongly disagreed; 18.2 % disagreed; 15.1 % were undecided; 33.9 % agreed; 21.2 % strongly agreed with the statement **"My manager congratulates me when I successfully fulfill my task"**. It was found that, the majority of the employees agreed with statement 11 and that their managers congratulated them when they successfully fulfilled their tasks.

Table 3.61 shows numerical distribution of the responds of the employees to the statement "My manager fully informs the employees about the work they will perform to make them successful in that work". It was found that, of the employees, 7.6 % strongly disagreed; 17 % disagreed; 15.4 % were undecided; 35.5 % agreed; 24.4 % strongly agreed with the statement **"My manager fully informs the employees about the work they will perform to make them successful in that work"**. It was found that, the majority of the employees agreed with statement 10 and that their managers fully informed their employees about the work they will perform to make them successful in their works. In other words, it can be stated that the managers gave importance to building accurate and effective communication with the employees to avoid making any mistakes at work.

Table 3.62 indicates numerical distribution of the responds of employees to the statement "My manager uses all means of communication he/she has for communication." It was found that, of the employees, 4.6 % strongly disagreed; 11.5 % disagreed; 11.8 % were undecided; 44.3 % agreed; 27.9 % strongly agreed with statement **"My manager uses all means of communication he/she has for communication."** It was found that the majority of the employees agreed with statement 13 and that their managers used all means of communication to communicate.

Table 3.62 Distribution of the responds of the participants to the statement "My manager uses all means of communication he/she has for communication."

13.	Statement	Frequency	Percentage	Mean	Standard deviation
	Strongly disagree	29	4.6		
	Disagree	72	11.5		
	Undecided	74	11.8	3.79	1.109
	Agree	278	44.3		
	Strongly agree	175	27.9		
	Total	628	100.0		

Table 3.63 Distribution of the responds of the participants to the statement "My manager is liked and respected by the employees

14.	Statement	Frequency	Percentage	Mean	Standard deviation
	Strongly disagree	42	6.7		
	Disagree	65	10.4		
	Undecided	122	19.4	3.68	1.179
	Agree	223	35.5		
	Strongly agree	176	28.0		
	Total	628	100.0		

Table 3.64 Distribution of the responds of the participants to the statement "My manager respects opinions and suggestions of the employees"

15.	Statement	Frequency	Percentage	Mean	Standard deviation
	Strongly disagree	48	7.6		
	Disagree	90	14.3		
	Undecided	120	19.1	3.55	1.226
	Agree	211	33.6		
	Strongly agree	159	25.3		
	Total	628	100.0		

Table 3.63 shows numerical distribution of the responds of the employees to the statement "My manager is liked and respected by the employees." It was found that, of the employees 6.7 % strongly disagreed; 10.4 % disagreed; 19.4 % were undecided; 35.5 % agreed; 28 % strongly agreed with the statement **"My manager is liked and respected by the employees."** It was found that the majority of the employees agreed with statement 14 and that their managers were liked and respected by their employees. In other words, it can be stated that the managers gained the respect of their employees thanks to their personality and behaviors in the work place.

Table 3.64 indicates numerical distribution of the responds of the employees to the statement "My manager respects opinions and suggestions of the employees." It was found that of the employees, 7.6 % strongly disagreed; 14.3 % disagreed; 19.1 % were undecided; 33.6 % agreed; 25.3 % strongly agreed with the statement **"My manager respects opinions and suggestions of the employees."** According

Table 3.65 Distribution of the responds of the participants to the statement "My manager checks whether the subordinates fully understood his/her orders by asking them questions"

16.	Statement	Frequency	Percentage	Mean	Standard deviation
	Strongly disagree	29	4.6		
	Disagree	93	14.8		
	Undecided	98	15.6	3.65	1.137
	Agree	254	40.4		
	Strongly agree	154	24.5		
	Total	628	100.0		

Table 3.66 Distribution of the responds of the participants to the statement "My manager creates an environment to allow the subordinates to express themselves"

17.	Statement	Frequency	Percentage	Mean	Standard deviation
	Strongly disagree	53	8.4		
	Disagree	103	16.4		
	Undecided	107	17.0	3.47	1.234
	Agree	228	36.3		
	Strongly agree	137	21.8		
	Total	628	100.0		

to these findings, the majority of the employees agreed with statement 15 and that their managers respected opinions and suggestions of their employees.

Table 3.65 shows numerical distribution of the responds of the employees to the statement "My manager checks whether the subordinates fully understood his/her orders by asking them questions." It was found that, of the employees, 4.6 % strongly disagreed; 14.8 disagreed; 15.6 % were undecided; 40.4 % agreed; 24.5 % strongly agreed the statement **"My manager checks whether the subordinates fully understood his/her orders by asking them questions."** It was found that the majority of the employees agreed with statement 16 and that their managers checked whether their orders were fully understood by their subordinates by asking them questions.

Table 3.66 indicates numerical distribution of the responds of the employees to the statement **"My manager creates an environment to allow the subordinates to express themselves."** It was found that, of the employees, 8.4 % strongly disagreed; 16.4 % disagreed; 17 % were undecided; 36.3 % agreed; 21.8 % strongly agreed with this statement. According to these findings, the majority of the employees agreed with statement 17 and that their managers created an environment to allow the subordinates to express themselves.

Table 3.67 presents numerical distribution of the responds of the employees to the statement "My manager makes clear, simple and understandable sentences while speaking to his/her subordinates." It was found that, of the employees, 4.9 % strongly disagreed; 12.7 % disagreed; 12.3 % were undecided; 42.5 % agreed; 27.5 % strongly agreed with the statement **"My manager makes clear, simple and understandable sentences while speaking to his/her subordinates."**

Table 3.67 Distribution of the responds of the participants to the statement "My manager makes clear, simple and understandable sentences while speaking to his/her subordinates"

18.	Statement	Frequency	Percentage	Mean	Standard deviation
	Strongly disagree	31	4.9		
	Disagree	80	12.7		
	Undecided	77	12.3	3.75	1.136
	Agree	267	42.5		
	Strongly agree	173	27.5		
	Total	628	100.0		

Table 3.68 Distribution of the responds of the participants to the statement "My manager establishes communication by taking the situations of the employees into account (by making empathy)"

19.	Statement	Frequency	Percentage	Mean	Standard deviation
	Strongly disagree	51	8.1		
	Disagree	102	16.2		
	Undecided	117	18.6	3.47	1.233
	Agree	215	34.2		
	Strongly agree	143	22.8		
	Total	628	100.0		

Table 3.69 Distribution of the responds of the participants to the statement "My manager uses body language (gestures and mimes) very well while speaking"

20.	Statement	Frequency	Percentage	Mean	Standard deviation
	Strongly disagree	40	6.4		
	Disagree	89	14.2		
	Undecided	98	15.6	3.64	1.196
	Agree	234	37.3		
	Strongly agree	167	26.6		
	Total	628	100.0		

It was found that the majority of the employees agreed with statement 18 and that their managers made clear, simple and understandable sentences while speaking to the subordinates.

Table 3.68 indicates numerical distribution of the responds of the employees to the statement "My manager establishes communication by taking the situations of the employees into account (by making empathy)". It was found that, of the employees, 8.1 %strongly disagreed; 16.2 % disagreed; 18.6 % were undecided; 34.2 % agreed; 22.8 % strongly agreed with the statement **"My manager establishes communication by taking the situations of the employees into account (by making empathy)"**. It was found that the majority of the employees agreed with statement 1 and that their managers established communication by taking the situations of the employees into account.

Table 3.70 Distribution of the responds of the participants to the statement "My manager uses time efficiently while communicating with his/her employees"

21	Statement	Frequency	Percentage	Mean	Standard deviation
	Strongly disagree	39	6.2		
	Disagree	76	12.1		
	Undecided	99	15.8	3.65	1.149
	Agree	264	42.0		
	Strongly agree	150	23.9		
	Total	628	100.0		

Table 3.71 Distribution of the responds of the participants to the statement "My manager makes eye contact with his/her employees while speaking"

22.	Statement	Frequency	Percentage	Mean	Standard deviation
	Strongly disagree	29	4.6		
	Disagree	60	9.6		
	Undecided	88	14.0	3.81	1.089
	Agree	274	43.6		
	Strongly agree	177	28.2		
	Total	628	100.0		

Table 3.69 shows numerical distribution of the responds of the employees to the statement "My manager uses body language (gestures and mimes) very well while speaking". It was found that of the employee, 6.4 % strongly disagreed; 14.2 % disagreed; 15.6 % were undecided; 37.3 % agreed; 26.6 % strongly agreed with the statement **"My manager uses body language (gestures and mimes) very well while speaking"**. According to these findings, it was found that the majority of the employees agreed with statement 20 and that their managers used body language very well while speaking.

Table 3.70 shows numerical distribution of the responds of the employees to the statement "My manager uses time efficiently while communicating with his/her employees." It was found that, of the employees, 6.2 % strongly disagreed; 12.1 % disagreed; 15.8 % were undecided; 42 % agreed; 23.9 % strongly agreed with the statement **"My manager uses time efficiently while communicating with his/her employees."** According to these findings, it was found that the majority of the employees agreed with statement 21 and that their managers used time efficiently while communicating with their employees.

Table 3.71 shows numerical distribution of the responds of the employees to the statement "My manager makes eye contact with his/her employees while speaking." It was found that of the employees, 6.2 % strongly disagreed; 12.1 % disagreed; 15.8 % were undecided; 42 % agreed; 23.9 % strongly agreed with the statement **"My manager makes eye contact with his/her employees while speaking."** According to this fining, it was found that the majority of the employees agreed with statement 12 and that their managers made eye contact while speaking.

Table 3.72 Distribution of the responds of the participants to the statement "My manager criticizes his/her employees without breaking his/her employees' hearts"

23.	Statement	Frequency	Percentage	Mean	Standard deviation
	Strongly disagree	79	12.6		
	Disagree	108	17.2		
	Undecided	91	14.5	3.37	1.342
	Agree	203	32.3		
	Strongly agree	147	23.4		
	Total	628	100.0		

Table 3.73 Distribution of the responds of the participants to the statement "My manager does not interrupt his/her employees unless necessary"

24.	Statement	Frequency	Percentage	Mean	Standard deviation
	Strongly disagree	68	10.8		
	Disagree	96	15.3		
	Undecided	96	15.3	3.45	1.291
	Agree	223	35.5		
	Strongly agree	145	23.1		
	Total	628	100.0		

Table 3.72 shows numerical distribution of the responds of the employees to the statement "My manager criticizes his/her employees without breaking his/her employees' hearts." It was found that, of the employees, 12.6 % strongly disagreed; 17.2 % disagreed; 14.5 % were undecided; 32.3 % agreed; 23.4 % strongly agreed with the statement **"My manager criticizes his/her employees without breaking his/her employees' hearts."** According to these findings, it was found that the majority of the employees agreed with statement 23 and that their managers criticized their employees without breaking their hearts and without demotivating them.

Table 3.73 shows numerical distribution of the responds of the employees to the statement "My manager does not interrupt his/her employees unless necessary". It was found that, of the employees, 10.8 % strongly disagreed; 15.3 % disagreed; 15.3 % were undecided; 35.5 % agreed; 23.1 % strongly agreed with the statement **"My manager does not interrupt his/her employees unless necessary".** According to these results, it was found that the majority of the employees agreed with statement 24 and that their managers did not interrupt their employees unless necessary and that they listened to them. This result might indicate that the managers respect their subordinates.

Table 3.74 shows numerical distribution of the responds of the employees to the statement "My manager does not criticize or say anything negative to his/her employees within a community". It was found that, of the employees, 14.% strongly disagreed; 15.8 % disagreed; 15.8 % were undecided; 31.2 % agreed, 22.8 % strongly disagreed with the statement **"My manager does not criticize or say anything negative to his/her employees within a community".** According to

Table 3.74 Distribution of the responds of the participants to the statement "My manager does not criticize or say anything negative to his/her employees within a community"

25.	Statement	Frequency	Percentage	Mean	Standard deviation
	Strongly disagree	91	14.5		
	Disagree	99	15.8		
	Undecided	99	15.8	3.32	1.364
	Agree	196	31.2		
	Strongly agree	143	22.8		
	Total	628	100.0		

these results the majority of the employees agreed with statement 25 and that their managers did not criticize or say anything negative to their employees within a community. In other words, it can be stated that the managers values emotions and opinions of their employees.

3.10   Evaluation and Interpretation of Study Findings

This section presents statistical analysis of study data. Mann-Whitney U test, Kruskal Wallis test and Tukey tests were applied to obtained data. The findings obtained from the analysis were then evaluated and presented in tables with various evaluations and interpretations.

3.10.1   Mann-Whitney Test Results of the Difference According to the Dimension of Marital Status

Mann-Whitney U test was performed to determine there was a difference between marital status of the employees; leadership behavior scale sub-dimensions and communication dimension. Test results are presented in Table 3.75. Since significance levels were found to be greater than 0.05 according to sub-dimensions of both scales ($p > 0.05$) it was found that there was no significant difference between marital status of the employees and leadership behaviors and communication sub-dimensions. According to this finding, our first hypothesis, H_1 was rejected and hypothesis H_0 was accepted. It was observed that there was no statistically significant difference between marital status, leadership behavior types and communication viewpoint of the employees. It can be stated that married or single status of the employees did not cause a difference between leadership behavior types and communication viewpoints.

Table 3.75 Mann-Whitney test results of the difference according to the dimension of marital status

Dimensions	Marital status	N	Mean	Sum of means
Employee-oriented	Married	524	316.47	165,514.50
	Single	104	301.57	31,363.50
	Total	628		
Task-oriented	Married	524	317.16	165,874.00
	Single	104	298.12	31,004.00
	Total	628		
Change-oriented	Married	524	317.72	166,487.50
	Single	104	298.25	31,018.50
	Total	628		
Communication	Married	524	318.05	166,657.50
	Single	104	296.62	30,848.50
	Total	628		
		Employee-oriented	Task-oriented	Change-oriented	Communication
Mann-Whitney U		25,903.500	25,544.000	25,558..000	25,388.500
Wilcoxon W		31,363.500	31,004.000	31,018..500	30,848.500
Z		−.767	−.981	−1..002	−1.101
Asymp. Sig. (2-tailed)		.443	.326	..326	271

Table 3.76 Mann-Whitney test results of the difference according to the dimension of working status of the spouses of the employees

Dimensions	Employment status of spouse	N	Mean	Sum of means
Employee O.	Working	229	258.81	59,009.50
	Not Working	289	259.15	74,893.50
	Total	518		
Task O.	Working	229	263.25	59,009.50
	Not Working	289	255.65	74,893.50
	Total	518		
Change O.	Working	229	267.33	61,219.00
	Not Working	289	253.29	73,202.00
	Total	518		
Communication	Working	229	264.30	60,524.50
	Not Working	289	255.70	73,896.50
	Total	518		
		Employee-oriented	Task-oriented	Change-oriented	Communication
Mann-Whitney U		32,903.500	31,976.500	31,297.000	31,991.500
Wilcoxon W		59,009.500	73,881.500	73,202.000	73,896.500
Z		−.025	−.576	−1.062	−.650
Asymp. Sig. (2-tailed)		.980	.565	.288	.516

Table 3.77 Kruskal Wallis test results of the difference according to dimension of age groups of the employees

Dimensions	Age Group	N	Mean
Employee O.	20–30	196	323.70
	31–40	301	307.61
	41–50	128	314.84
	51 and above	3	284.00
	Total	628	
Task O.	20–30	196	320.23
	31–40	301	306.33
	41–50	128	322.78
	51 and above	3	299.17
	Total	628	
Change O.	20–30	196	328.69
	31–40	301	305.11
	41–50	128	314.42
	51 and above	3	333.00
	Total	628	
Communication D.	20–30	196	323.19
	31–40	301	307.70
	41–50	128	317.49
	51 and above	3	301.00
	Total	628	

	Employee-oriented	Task-oriented	Change-oriented	Communication
Chi-Square	1.023	1.095	2.045	.925
df	3	3	3	3
Asymp. Sig.	.796	.778	.563	.819

3.10.2   Mann-Whitney Test Results of the Difference According to the Dimension of Working Status of the Spouses of the Employees

Mann-Whitney U test was performed to determine whether there was a difference between working status of the spouses of the employees; leadership behavior scale sub-dimensions and communication dimension. Test results are presented in Table 3.76. Since significance levels were found to be greater than 0.05 according to sub-dimensions of both scales ($p > 0.05$) it was found that there was no significant difference between working status of the spouses of the employees and leadership behaviors and communication sub-dimensions. According to this finding, our second hypothesis, H_1 was rejected and hypothesis H_0 was accepted. It was observed that there was no statistically significant difference between working status of the spouses of the employees, leadership behavior types and communication viewpoint of the employees. It can be stated whether the spouses of the employees were working or not working did not cause a difference between leadership behavior types and communication viewpoints.

Table 3.78 Kruskal Wallis test results of the difference according to dimension of seniority of the employees

Dimensions	Seniority (year)	N		Mean
Employee O.	1–10	335		304.12
	11–20	233		323.15
	21–30	58		332.04
	31 and above	2		376.00
	Total	628		
Task O.	1–10	335		307.33
	11–20	233		319.27
	21–30	58		329.09
	31 and above	2		376.75
	Total	628		
Change O.	1–10	335		309.73
	11–20	233		318.47
	21–30	58		322.54
	31 and above	2		418.00
	Total	628		
Communication D.	1–10	335		306.35
	11–20	233		323.89
	21–30	58		322.28
	31 and above	2		360.25
	Total	628		
	Employee-oriented	Task-oriented	Change-oriented	Communication
Chi-Square	2.404	1.298	1.114	1.536
df	3	3	3	3
Asymp. Sig.	.493	.730	.774	.674

Kruskal Wallis test was performed to determine whether there was a difference between leadership behavior sub-dimension and communication dimension according to age group of the employees. Test results are presented in Table 3.77. Since significance levels were found to be greater than 0.05 according to sub-dimensions of both scales ($p > 0.05$) it was found that there was no significant difference between age groups of the employees and leadership behaviors and communication sub-dimensions. According to this finding, our third hypothesis H_1 was rejected and hypothesis H_0 was accepted. It was observed that there was no statistically significant difference between age groups, leadership behavior types and communication viewpoint of the employees. It can be stated that there was no significant difference between leadership behavior types and communication view-points of the employees from different age groups.

Kruskal Wallis test was performed to determine whether there was a difference between leadership behavior sub-dimensions and communication dimension according to the seniority of the employees. Test results are presented in Table 3.78. Since significance levels were found to be greater than 0.05 according to sub-dimensions of both scales ($p > 0.05$) it was found that there was no significant

Table 3.79 Mann-Whitney test results of the difference according to the dimension of gender of the employees

Dimensions	Gender	N	Mean	Sum of means
Employee O.	Female	163	338.01	54,757.00
	Male	465	305.64	142,121.00
	Total	628		
Task-oriented	Female	163	347.40	56,278.50
	Male	465	302.36	140,599.50
	Total	628		
Change O.	Female	163	353.81	57,671.00
	Male	465	300.72	139,835.00
	Total	628		
Communication	Female	163	349.75	57,009.00
	Male	465	302.14	140,497.00
	Total	628		
		Employee-oriented	Task-oriented	Change-oriented	Communication
Mann-Whitney U		33,776.000	32,254.500	31,490.000	32,152.000
Wilcoxon W		142,121.000	140,599.500	139,835.000	140,497.000
Z		−1.961	−2.731	−3.222	−2.885
Significance Level		.050	.006	.001	.004

difference between seniority levels of the employees, leadership behaviors and communication sub-dimensions. According to this finding, our fourth hypothesis H_1 was rejected and hypothesis H_0 was accepted. It was observed that there was no statistically significant difference between seniority levels, leadership behavior types and communication viewpoint of the employees. It can be stated that there was no significant difference between leadership behavior types and communication viewpoints of the employees having different seniority levels.

3.10.3   Mann-Whitney Test Results of the Difference according to the Dimension of Gender of the Employees

Mann-Whitney U test was performed to determine whether there was a difference between leadership behavior sub-dimensions and communication dimension according to the seniority of the employees. Test results are presented in Table 3.79. Since significance levels were found to be smaller than 0.05 according to sub-dimensions of both scales ($p < 0.05$) it was found that there was a difference between employee-oriented, task-oriented, change-oriented leadership behavior sub-dimensions according to the genders of the employees. In addition, it was found that there was a difference in communication scale dimension. According to this finding, our fifth hypothesis H_0 was rejected and hypothesis H_1 was accepted. It was observed that there was a statistically significant difference between genders, leadership behavior types and communication viewpoint of the employees.

Based on this finding, when compared to female employees, male employees had a more positive opinion about leadership behaviors and communication process of their managers. In other words, male employees defined their managers as more employee-oriented, task oriented and change-oriented leaders than female employees. Furthermore, male employees had a different viewpoint than female employees about communication dimension of their managers. According to this finding, it can be stated that gender was a variable which caused different perceptions of leadership behavior types and communication process. In other words, when compared to female employees, male employees find their managers more successful in communication process.

3.10.4 Kruskal Wallis Test Results of the Difference According to the Dimension of Working Sectors of the Employees

Kruskal Wallis test was performed to determine whether there was a difference between leadership behavior sub-dimensions and communication dimension according to the working sectors of the employees. Test results are presented in Table 3.80. Since significance levels were found to be smaller than 0.05 according to sub-dimensions of both scales ($p < 0.05$) it was found that there was a difference between employee-oriented, task-oriented, change-oriented leadership behavior sub-dimensions and communication dimension according to the working sectors of the employees. According to this finding, our sixth hypothesis H_0 was rejected and hypothesis H_1 was accepted. It was observed that there was a statistically significant difference between working sectors, leadership behavior types and communication viewpoint of the employees.

Tukey test was performed to determine the sector which caused this difference. Test results are presented in Table 3.81. Significance level in Tukey HSD multiple comparison table can be used to find the sector which cause the difference. Test results showed that the employees working in glass sector perceived their managers as more employee-oriented than those in textile sector and that the employees working in apparel sector perceived their managers more employee-oriented than those in textile sector. Similarly, the employees working in glass sector perceived their managers more task-oriented than those in textile sector and that the employees working in apparel sector perceived their managers more task-oriented than those in textile sector.

In addition, the employees working in glass sector perceived their managers as more change-oriented than those in textile sector and that the employees working in

Table 3.80 Kruskal Wallis test results of the difference according to the dimension of working sectors of the employees

Dimensions	Sector	N	Mean
Employee O.	Glass	225	376.64
	Apparel	152	222.10
	Textile	221	342.73
	Total	628	
Task O.	Glass	225	375.63
	Apparel	152	215.70
	Textile	221	353.79
	Total	628	
Change O.	Glass	225	365.14
	Apparel	152	227.07
	Textile	221	356.66
	Total	628	
Communication	Glass	225	371.18
	Apparel	152	219.43
	Textile	221	357.63
	Total	628	
	Employee oriented	Task oriented	Change-oriented	Communication
Chi-Square	91.389	102.333	79.744	94.319
df	2	2	2	2
Asymp. Sig.	.000	.000	.000	.000

apparel sector perceived their managers as more change-oriented than those in textile sector. On the other hand, the employees working in glass sector found their managers more successful in communication process than those in textile sector and that the employees working in apparel sector found their managers more successful in communication process than those in textile sector. In general terms, when compared to the employees working other sectors, the employees working in glass sector defined their managers as employee-oriented, task-oriented and change-oriented.

An employee-oriented leader values the employers; motivates them by establishing good communication with them; enables them to succeed in their tasks; has a positive attitude towards assignment of authority; increases job satisfaction of group members; pays attention to improving and development of working conditions and pays attention to self-development of the employees. A task-oriented leader values rules and working; gives secondary importance to employees; inspects whether group members work according to previously determined rules and standards and mostly uses formal power based on position (Çetin and Beceren 2007:127). On the other hand, change-oriented a leader questions existing working conditions; environment and structure and wishes for continuous change and development at the workplace. He/she pioneers attempts of desired change in an organization; shows behaviors to change the structure of the organization and gives a vision to the employees (Şahin and Gül 2011:241–242).

The fact that the managers in glass sector show different leadership behavior types (employee-oriented, task-oriented and change-oriented) according to

Table 3.81 Tukey HSD multiple comparison table

Dimensions	(I) Sector	(J) Dimensions	Mean Difference (I–J)	Std. Error	Sig.
Employee O.	Glass		11.60422[a]	1.20938	.000
	Textile	Apparel	2.92393	1.35123	.078
	Textile	**Glass**	−11.60422[a]	1.20938	.000
		Apparel	−8.68029[a]	1.38935	.000
	Apparel	**Glass**	−2.92393	1.35123	.078
		Textile	8.68029[a]	1.38935	.000
Task O.	**Glass**	**Textile**	9.08537[a]	.89040	.000
		Apparel	1.55086	.99484	.264
	Textile	**Glass**	−9.08537[a]	.89040	.000
		Apparel	−7.53451[a]	1.02290	.000
	Apparel	**Glass**	−1.55086	.99484	.264
		Textile	7.53451[a]	1.02290	.000
Change O.	**Glass**	**Textile**	6.86184[a]	.79563	.000
		Apparel	.66894	.88712	.731
	Textile	**Glass**	−6.86184[a]	.79563	.000
		Apparel	−6.19290[a]	.91225	.000
	Apparel	**Glass**	−.66894	.88712	.731
		Textile	6.19290[a]	.91225	.000
Communication	**Glass**	**Textile**	20.98492[a]	2.16205	.000
		Apparel	2.36545	2.41065	.589
	Textile	**Glass**	−20.98492[a]	2.16205	.000
		Apparel	−18.61946[a]	2.47894	.000
	Apparel	**Glass**	−2.36545	2.41065	.589
		Textile	18.61946[a]	2.47894	.000

[a]The mean difference is significant at the .05 level

conditions might be caused by the strong and dynamic structure of this sector. Furthermore, the fact that effective communication is necessary between the employees and managers to be effective in this sector can be shown as a reason for perception of the managers as successful in communication dimension by the employees. On the other hand, employee-oriented, task-oriented and change-oriented leadership behavior can be considered as a situation which requires a leader to establish a good level of communication with his/her subordinates. A leader cooperates with his/her employees by building good communication with them and can transfer their tasks, goals to be fulfilled and the existing changing process effectively.

3.10.5   Kruskal Wallis Test Results of the Difference According to the Dimension of Income Levels of the Employees

Kruskal Wallis test was performed to determine whether there was a difference between leadership behavior sub-dimensions and communication dimension

Table 3.82 Kruskal Wallis test results of the difference according to the dimension of income levels of the employees

Dimensions	Income	N		Mean
Employee O.	700 and below	56		263.32
	701–2,200	544		314.67
	2,201–3,700	23		414.02
	3,701 and above	5		348.30
	Total	628		
Task O.	700 and below	56		267.54
	701–2,200	544		313.28
	2,201–3,700	23		430.67
	3,701 and above	5		376.30
	Total	628		
Change O.	700 and below	56		278.13
	701–2,200	544		313.50
	2,201–3,700	23		421.09
	3,701 and above	5		340.10
	Total	628		
Communication D.	700 and below	56		264.20
	701–2,200	544		314.89
	2,201–3,700	23		405.41
	3,701 and above	5		417.20
	Total	628		
	Employee-oriented	Task-oriented	Change-oriented	Communication
Chi-Square	11.610	13.886	10.350	11.705
df	3	3	3	3
Asymp. Sig.	.009	.003	.016	.008

according to the income groups of the employees. Test results are presented in Table 3.82. Since significance levels were found to be smaller than 0.05 according to sub-dimensions of both scales ($p < 0.05$) it was found that there was a significant difference between income groups of the employees, employee-oriented, task-oriented and change-oriented leadership behaviors and communication sub-dimensions. According to this finding, our seventh hypothesis, H_0 was rejected and hypothesis H_1 was accepted. It was observed that there was a statistically significant difference between income levels, leadership behavior types and communication viewpoint of the employees.

Tukey test was performed to determine the income group which caused this difference. Test results are presented in Table 3.83. It was found that when compared to the employees in 700 TL and below income group, the employees in 2,201–3,700 TL income group found their leaders as more employee-oriented leaders. Similarly, when compared to the employees in 700 TL and below income group and 701–2,200 TL income group, the employees in 2,201–3,700 TL income group perceived their employees as more task-oriented leaders. Similarly, when compared to the employees in 700 TL and below income group and the employees in 701–2,200 TL income group, the employees in 2,201–3,700 TL income group

Table 3.83 Tukey HSD multiple comparison table

Dimensions	(I) Income range	(J) Income range	Mean difference (I–J)	Std. error	Sig.
Employee O.	700 and below	701–2,200	−4.23780	1.96880	.138
		2,201–3,700	−11.13587[a]	3.47406	.008
		3,701 and above	−5.67500	6.54738	.822
	701–2,200	700 and below	4.23780	1.96880	.138
		2,201–3,700	−6.89807	2.98625	.097
		3,701 and above	−1.43720	6.30212	.996
	2,201–3,700	700 and below	11.13587[a]	3.47406	.008
		701–2,200	6.89807	2.98625	.097
		3,701 and above	5.46087	6.92168	.859
	3,701 and above	700 and below	5.67500	6.54738	.822
		701–2,200	1.43720	6.30212	.996
		2,201–3,700	−5.46087	6.92168	.859
Task O.	700 and below	701–2,200	−2.69794	1.46260	.253
		2,201–3,700	−9.54581[a]	2.58084	.001
		3,701 and above	−4.58929	4.86398	.781
	701–2,200	700 and below	2.69794	1.46260	.253
		2,201–3,700	−6.84787[a]	2.21846	.011
		3,701 and above	−1.89134	4.68179	.978
	2,201–3,700	700 and below	9.54581[a]	2.58084	.001
		701–2,200	6.84787[a]	2.21846	.011
		3,701 and above	4.95652	5.14205	.770
	3,701 and above	700 and below	4.58929	4.86398	.781
		701–2,200	1.89134	4.68179	.978
		2,201–3,700	−4.95652	5.14205	.770
Change O.	700 and below	701–2,200	−1.76366	1.28491	.517
		2,201–3,700	−7.13898[a]	2.26749	.009
		3,701 and above	−2.06071	4.27343	.963
	701–2,200	700 and below	1.76366	1.28491	.517
		2,201–3,700	−5.37532[a]	1.94903	.030
		3,701 and above	−.29706	4.11332	1.000
	2,201–3,700	700 and below	7.13898[a]	2.26749	.009
		701–2,200	5.37532[a]	1.94903	.030
		3,701 and above	5.07826	4.51773	.675
	3,701 and above	700 and below	2.06071	4.27343	.963
		701–2,200	.29706	4.11332	1.000
		2,201–3,700	−5.07826	4.51773	.675
Communication	700 and below	701–2,200	−7.01943	3.54008	.196
		2,201–3,700	−19.81211[a]	6.24721	.009
		3,701 and above	−19.06429	11.77380	.368
	701–2,200	700 and below	7.01943	3.54008	.196
		2,201–3,700	−12.79268	5.36981	.082
		3,701 and above	−12.04485	11.33267	.712
	2,201–3,700	700 and below	19.81211[a]	6.24721	.009
		701–2,200	12.79268	5.36981	.082
		3,701 and above	.74783	12.44689	1.000

(continued)

Table 3.83 (continued)

Dimensions	(I) Income range	(J) Income range	Mean difference (I–J)	Std. error	Sig.
	3,701 and above	700 and below	19.06429	11.77380	.368
		701–2,200	12.04485	11.33267	.712
		2,201–3,700	−.74783	12.44689	1.000

[a]The mean difference is significant at the .05 level

perceived their managers as more change-oriented leaders. In terms of communication scale, the employees in 2,201–3,700 TL income group found their managers more successful in communication process than those in 700 TL income group. Based on these findings, it can be stated that the employees in high income group had different perceptions of leadership behavior types and communication dimension then the employees in low income group. In other words, it can be stated that the employees in high income level found their managers more successful in communication process than those in low income group.

3.10.6 Kruskal Wallis Test Results of the Difference According to the Dimension of Place of Upbringing of the Employees

Kruskal Wallis test was performed to determine whether there was a difference between leadership behavior sub-dimensions and communication dimension according to place of upbringing of the employees. Test results are presented in Table 3.84. Since significance levels were found to be smaller than 0.05 according to sub-dimensions of both scales ($p < 0.05$) it was found that there was a significant difference between employee-oriented, task-oriented and change-oriented leadership behaviors and communication sub-dimensions of the employees according to their places of upbringing. According to this finding, our eighth hypothesis H_0 was rejected and hypothesis H_1 was accepted. It was observed that there was a statistically significant difference between place of upbringing, leadership behavior types and communication viewpoint of the employees.

Tukey test was performed to determine the place of upbringing which caused this difference. Test results are presented in Table 3.85. Test results showed that when compared to the employees who grew up in villages or cities, the employees who grew up in large cities perceived their managers as task-oriented leaders. Similarly, when compared to the employees who grew up in villages, the employees who grew up in districts found their managers as task-oriented. On the other hand, when compared to the employees who grew up in villages, the employees who grew up in large cities found their managers more successful in communication. In other words, the employees who grew up in large cities considered their leaders as the ones who can establish good communication with them. On the other hand, the

Table 3.84 Kruskal Wallis Test results of the difference according to the dimension of place of upbringing of the employees

Dimensions	Place of Upbringing	N			Mean
Employee O.		247			298.93
	Village	35			319.26
	Town	119			353.95
	District	204			298.64
	City	23			396.72
	Total	628			
Task O.		247			299.00
	Village	35			328.00
	Town	119			354.34
	District	204			294.50
	City	23			417.33
	Total	628			
Change O.		247			304.63
	Village	35			314.36
	Town	119			347.59
	District	204			297.20
	City	23			402.91
	Total	628			
Communication		247			302.31
	Village	35			322.59
	Town	119			346.07
	District	204			298.29
	City	23			413.46
	Total	628			
	Employee-oriented	Task-oriented	Change-oriented	Communication	
Chi-Square	13.817	17.720	12.059	13.280	
df	4	4	4	4	
Asymp. Sig.	.008	.001	.017	.010	

employees who grew up in large cities defined their managers as employee, task and change-oriented. According to these findings, it can be stated that the employees who grew up in large cities had a different perception of leadership behavior types and communication dimension. In short, when compared to the employees who grew up in other places, the employees who grew up in large cities found their managers more successful in communication process. The fact that the employees who grew up in large cities are more advantageous than those who grew up in other places in terms of social interaction and that they develop themselves in terms of communication might be a cause of this result.

Table 3.85 Tukey HSD multiple comparison table

Dimensions	(I) Place of upbringing	(J) Place of upbringing	Mean difference (I–J)	Std. error	Sig.
Employee O.	*Village*	*Town*	−1.80116	2.53039	.954
		District	−4.18603	1.56338	.058
		City	.15155	1.32726	1.000
		Large City	−7.11917	3.05433	.137
	Town	Village	1.80116	2.53039	.954
		District	−2.38487	2.69401	.902
		City	1.95271	2.56420	.941
		Large City	−5.31801	3.76064	.619
	District	Village	4.18603	1.56338	.058
		Town	2.38487	2.69401	.902
		City	4.33758	1.61753	.058
		Large City	−2.93314	3.19119	.890
	City	Village	−.15155	1.32726	1.000
		Town	−1.95271	2.56420	.941
		District	−4.33758	1.61753	.058
		Large City	−7.27072	3.08239	.128
	Large City	Village	7.11917	3.05433	.137
		Town	5.31801	3.76064	.619
		District	2.93314	3.19119	.890
		City	7.27072	3.08239	.128
Task O.	Village	Town	−1.61347	1.87743	.912
		District	−3.37146[a]	1.16043	.031
		City	.40375	.98409	.994
		Large City	−6.39484[a]	2.26599	.039
	Town	*Village*	1.61347	1.87743	.912
		District	−1.75798	1.99832	.904
		City	2.01723	1.90135	.826
		Town	−4.78137	2.78952	.426
	District	Village	3.37146[a]	1.16043	.031
		Town	1.75798	1.99832	.904
		City	3.77521[a]	1.19874	.015
		Large City	−3.02338	2.36712	.705
	City	Village	−.40375	.98409	.994
		Town	−2.01723	1.90135	.826
		District	−3.77521[a]	1.19874	.015
		Large City	−6.79859[a]	2.28585	.025
	Large City	Village	6.39484[a]	2.26599	.039
		Town	4.78137	2.78952	.426
		District	3.02338	2.36712	.705
		City	6.79859[a]	2.28585	.025
Change O.	Village	Town	−.96437	1.65150	.977
		District	−2.33076	1.02036	.151
		City	.47876	.86509	.982
		Large City	−4.62524	1.99345	.140

(continued)

Table 3.85 (continued)

Dimensions	(I) Place of upbringing	(J) Place of upbringing	Mean difference (I−J)	Std. error	Sig.
	Town	Village	.96437	1.65150	.977
		District	−1.36639	1.75829	.937
		City	1.44314	1.67296	.910
		Large City	−3.66087	2.45444	.568
	District	Village	2.33076	1.02036	.151
		Town	1.36639	1.75829	.937
		City	2.80952	1.05475	.061
		Large City	−2.29448	2.08278	.806
	City	Village	−.47876	.86509	.982
		Town	−1.44314	1.67296	.910
		District	−2.80952	1.05475	.061
		Large City	−5.10401	2.01127	.084
	Large City	Village	4.62524	1.99345	.140
		Town	3.66087	2.45444	.568
		District	2.29448	2.08278	.806
		City	5.10401	2.01127	.084
Communication	Village	Town	−2.70573	4.55241	.976
		District	−5.93934	2.81267	.216
		City	.90240	2.38465	.996
		Large City	−15.26597[a]	5.49502	.045
	Town	Village	2.70573	4.55241	.976
		District	−3.23361	4.84677	.963
		City	3.60812	4.61158	.936
		Large City	−12.56025	6.76574	.342
	District	Village	5.93934	2.81267	.216
		Town	3.23361	4.84677	.963
		City	6.84174	2.90745	.130
		Large City	−9.32664	5.74125	.482
	City	Village	−.90240	2.38465	.996
		Town	−3.60812	4.61158	.936
		District	−6.84174	2.90745	.130
		Large City	−16.16837[a]	5.54413	.030
	Large City	Village	15.26597[a]	5.49502	.045
		Town	12.56025	6.76574	.342
		District	9.32664	5.74125	.482
		City	16.16837[a]	5.54413	.030

[a]The mean difference is significant at the .05 level

3.10.7 Kruskal Wallis Test Results of the Difference According to the Dimension of Educational Level of the Employees

Kruskal Wallis test was performed to determine there was a difference between leadership behavior sub-dimensions and communication dimension according to

Table 3.86 Kruskal Wallis Test results of the difference according to the dimension of educational level of the employees

Dimensions	Educational Status	N	Mean
Employee O.	Primary school	118	259.83
	Secondary school	74	272.57
	High school	360	323.29
	2-Year degree	68	402.07
	Bachelor's degree	8	330.63
	Total	628	
Task O.	Primary school	117	261.74
	Secondary school	74	287.61
	High school	360	319.12
	2-Year degree	68	406.69
	Bachelor's degree	8	304.25
	Total	628	
Change O.	Primary school	118	276.27
	Secondary school	74	279.01
	High school	360	319.33
	2-Year degree	68	398.65
	Bachelor's degree	8	274.19
	Total	628	
Communication D.	Primary school	118	271.19
	Secondary school	74	268.00
	High school	360	320.98
	2-Year degree	68	404.65
	Bachelor's degree	8	325.75
	Total	628	

	Employee-oriented	Task-oriented	Change-oriented	Communication
Chi-Square	31.587	29.552	23.451	28.916
df	4	4	4	4
Asymp. Sig.	.000	.000	.000	.000

educational level of the employees. Test results are presented in Table 3.86. Since significance levels were found to be smaller than 0.05 according to sub-dimensions of both scales ($p < 0.05$) it was found that there was a significant difference between employee-oriented, task-oriented and change-oriented leadership behavior sub-dimensions and communication sub-dimensions of the employees according to their educational levels. According to this finding, our ninth hypothesis H_0 was rejected and hypothesis H_1 was accepted. It was observed that there was a statistically significant difference between educational level, leadership behavior types and communication viewpoint of the employees.

Tukey test was performed to determine the educational level which caused this difference. Test results are resented in Table 3.87. Test results showed that when compared to the employees who were primary school, secondary school and high school graduates, the employees who had 2-year degree perceived their managers as employee-oriented leaders. Similarly, when compared to the employees who

Table 3.87 Tukey HSD multiple comparison table

Dimensions	(I) Place of upbringing	(J) Place of upbringing	Mean difference (I–J)	Std. error	Sig.
Employee O.	Primary school	Secondary school	−1.34127	2.04376	.965
		High school	−4.85260[a]	1.46254	.008
		2-Year degree	−11.54636[a]	2.09845	.000
		Bachelor's degree	−6.01695	5.03543	.754
	Secondary school	Primary school	1.34127	2.04376	.965
		High school	−3.51133	1.75962	.269
		2-Year degree	−10.20509[a]	2.31532	.000
		Bachelor's degree	−4.67568	5.12960	.892
	High school	Primary school	4.85260[a]	1.46254	.008
		Secondary school	3.51133	1.75962	.269
		2-Year degree	−6.69376[a]	1.82284	.002
		Bachelor's degree	−1.16435	4.92695	.999
	2-Year degree	Primary school	11.54636[a]	2.09845	.000
		Secondary school	10.20509[a]	2.31532	.000
		High school	6.69376[a]	1.82284	.002
		Bachelor's degree	5.52941	5.15163	.820
	Bachelor's degree	Primary school	6.01695	5.03543	.754
		Secondary school	4.67568	5.12960	.892
		High school	1.16435	4.92695	.999
		2-Year degree	−5.52941	5.15163	.820
Task O.	Primary school	Secondary school	−1.38311	1.52637	.895
		High school	−3.18462[a]	1.09362	.030
		2-Year degree	−8.69671[a]	1.56707	.000
		Bachelor's degree	−2.20406	3.75550	.977
	Secondary school	Primary school	1.38311	1.52637	.895
		High school	−1.80150	1.31168	.645
		2-Year degree	−7.31359[a]	1.72634	.000
		Bachelor's degree	−.82095	3.82470	1.000
	High school	Primary school	3.18462[a]	1.09362	.030
		Secondary school	1.80150	1.31168	.645
		2-Year degree	−5.51209[a]	1.35884	.001
		Bachelor's degree	.98056	3.67349	.999
	2-Year degree	Primary school	8.69671[a]	1.56707	.000
		Secondary school	7.31359[a]	1.72634	.000
		High school	5.51209[a]	1.35884	.001
		Bachelor's degree	6.49265	3.84113	.441
	Bachelor's degree	Primary school	2.20406	3.75550	.977
		Secondary school	.82095	3.82470	1.000
		High school	−.98056	3.67349	.999
		2-Year degree	−6.49265	3.84113	.441
Change O.	Primary school	Secondary school	−.25630	1.34250	1.000
		High school	−2.21163	.96037	.145
		2-Year degree	−6.46735[a]	1.37842	.000
		Bachelor's degree	−.86441	3.30764	.999
	Secondary school	Primary school	.25630	1.34250	1.000

(continued)

Table 3.87 (continued)

Dimensions	(I) Place of upbringing	(J) Place of upbringing	Mean difference (I–J)	Std. error	Sig.
		High school	−1.95533	1.15557	.440
		2-Year degree	−6.21105[a]	1.52087	.000
		Bachelor's degree	−.60811	3.36950	1.000
	High school	Primary school	2.21163	.96037	.145
		Secondary school	1.95533	1.15557	.440
		2-Year degree	−4.25572[a]	1.19711	.004
		Bachelor's degree	1.34722	3.23629	.994
	2-Year degree	Primary school	6.46735[a]	1.37842	.000
		Secondary school	6.21105[a]	1.52087	.000
		High school	4.25572[a]	1.19711	.004
		Bachelor's degree	5.60294	3.38397	.462
	Bachelor's degree	Primary school	.86441	3.30764	.999
		Secondary school	.60811	3.36950	1.000
		High school	−1.34722	3.23629	.994
		2-Year degree	−5.60294	3.38397	.462
Communication	Primary school	Secondary school	.50183	3.68411	1.000
		High school	−6.61874	2.63548	.089
		2-Year degree	−19.35469[a]	3.78268	.000
		Bachelor's degree	−9.45763	9.07691	.836
	Secondary school	Primary school	−.50183	3.68411	1.000
		High school	−7.12057	3.17115	.165
		2-Year degree	−19.85652[a]	4.17362	.000
		Bachelor's degree	−9.95946	9.24666	.818
	High school	Primary school	6.61874	2.63548	.089
		Secondary school	7.12057	3.17115	.165
		2-Year degree	−12.73595[a]	3.28515	.001
		Bachelor's degree	−2.83889	8.88109	.998
	2-Year degree	Primary school	19.35469[a]	3.78268	.000
		Secondary school	19.85652[a]	4.17362	.000
		High school	12.73595[a]	3.28515	.001
		Bachelor's degree	9.89706	9.28637	.824
	Bachelor's degree	Primary school	9.45763	9.07691	.836
		Secondary school	9.95946	9.24666	.818
		High school	2.83889	8.88109	.998
		2-Year degree	−9.89706	9.28637	.824

[a]The mean difference is significant at the .05 level

graduated from primary school, high school graduates found their managers as employee-oriented leaders. When compared to primary school, secondary school and high school graduates, the employees with 2-year degree perceived their leaders as change-oriented leaders. On the other hand, when compared to primary school, secondary school and high school graduates, the employees with 2-year degree found their managers more effective in communication process.

In general terms, it was found that when compared to the employees with low educational level, the employees with high educational level had different perceptions of leadership behaviors of their managers. As a result, high educational level can be considered as a variable which caused different perception of leadership behaviors. The same comment is valid for communication process. In other words, the employees with high educational level found their managers more effective and successful in communication. Furthermore, high educational level can be considered as a situation which causes different perceptions of the employees about the same situation.

3.10.8 Kruskal Wallis Test Results of the Difference According to the Dimension of Educational Level of Mother of the Employees

Kruskal Wallis test was performed to determine if there was a difference between leadership behavior sub-dimensions and communication dimension according to educational levels of mothers of the employees. Test results are presented in Table 3.88. Since significance levels were found to be smaller than 0.05 according to sub-dimensions of both scales ($p < 0.10$) it was found that there was a significant difference between employee-oriented, task-oriented and change-oriented leadership behavior sub-dimensions and communication sub-dimensions of the employees according to their educational levels. According to this finding, our tenth hypothesis, H_0 was rejected and hypothesis H_1 was accepted. It was observed that there was a statistically significant difference between educational level of mothers of the employees, leadership behavior types and communication viewpoint of the employees.

Tukey test was performed to determine the educational level which caused this difference. Test results are presented in Table 3.89. It was found that when compared to the employees whose mothers were illiterate, the employees whose mothers were university graduates perceived their managers as employee-oriented. It was found that when compared to the employees whose mothers were illiterate, primary school, secondary school or high school graduates, the employees whose mothers were university graduates perceived their managers as task-oriented leaders. When compared to the employees whose mothers were illiterate, primary school, secondary school or high school graduates, the employees whose mothers were university graduates perceived their managers as change-oriented leaders. On the other hand, it was found that when compared to the employees whose mothers were illiterate, primary school, secondary school or high school graduates, the employees whose mothers were university graduates perceived their managers more successful in communication process.

In general terms, it can be stated that the employees whose mothers had a high educational level had a different perception of leadership behaviors of their leaders

Table 3.88 Kruskal Wallis Test Results of the Difference according to the Dimension of Educational Level of Mother of the Employees

Dimensions	Educational status of mother	N	Mean
Employee O.	Illiterate	81	284.08
	Primary school	452	313.93
	Secondary school	54	325.73
	High school	39	346.54
	University	32	590.00
	Total	628	
Task O.	Illiterate	81	290.20
	Primary school	452	313.19
	Secondary school	54	314.51
	High school	39	357.17
	University	2	606.00
	Total	628	
Change O.	Illiterate	81	289.97
	Primary school	452	312.79
	Secondary school	54	325.47
	High school	39	354.36
	University	2	620.50
	Total	628	
Communication D.	Illiterate	81	279.07
	Primary school	452	314.88
	Secondary school	54	325.19
	High school	39	352.96
	University	2	626.00
	Total	628	
	Employee-oriented	Task-oriented	Change-oriented	Communication
Chi-Square	8.358	8.859	9.331	10.946
df	4	4	4	4
Asymp. Sig.	.079	.065	.053	.027

when compared to the employees whose mothers had a low educational level. Based on these findings, high educational status of mother can be considered as a variable which causes different perceptions of leadership behaviors. Similarly, it can be stated that the employees whose mothers had a high educational level found their managers more successful in communication process. As a result, high educational level can be considered as an important variable in perceiving leadership behaviors and communication effectiveness. It can be stated that the individuals who were reared by mothers with a high educational level will have different perspectives.

Table 3.89 Tukey HSD multiple comparison table

Dimensions	(I) Educational status of mother	(J) Educational status of mother	Mean difference (I–J)	Std. error	Sig.
Employee O.	Illiterate	Primary school	−1.97895	1.69536	.770
		Secondary school	−2.43210	2.46812	.862
		High school	−4.06173	2.73813	.574
		University	−28.72840[a]	10.05587	.036
	Primary school	Illiterate	1.97895	1.69536	.770
		Secondary school	−.45315	2.02301	.999
		High school	−2.08278	2.34485	.901
		University	−26.74945	9.95597	.057
	Secondary school	Illiterate	2.43210	2.46812	.862
		Primary school	.45315	2.02301	.999
		High school	−1.62963	2.95223	.982
		University	−26.29630	10.11626	.072
	High school	Illiterate	4.06173	2.73813	.574
		Primary school	2.08278	2.34485	.901
		Secondary school	1.62963	2.95223	.982
		University	−24.66667	10.18550	.111
	University	Illiterate	28.72840[a]	10.05587	.036
		Primary school	26.74945	9.95597	.057
		Secondary school	26.29630	10.11626	.072
		High school	24.66667	10.18550	.111
Task O.	Illiterate	Primary school	−1.19597	1.25698	.876
		Secondary school	−1.14198	1.82991	.971
		High school	−4.05793	2.03010	.268
		University	−26.16049[a]	7.45561	.004
	Primary school	Illiterate	1.19597	1.25698	.876
		Secondary school	.05400	1.49990	1.000
		High school	−2.86196	1.73852	.468
		University	−24.96452[a]	7.38155	.007
	Secondary school	Illiterate	1.14198	1.82991	.971
		Primary school	−.05400	1.49990	1.000
		High school	−2.91595	2.18884	.671
		University	−25.01852[a]	7.50039	.008
	High school	Illiterate	4.05793	2.03010	.268
		Primary school	2.86196	1.73852	.468
		Secondary school	2.91595	2.18884	.671
		University	−22.10256[a]	7.55173	.029
	University	Illiterate	26.16049[a]	7.45561	.004
		Primary school	24.96452[a]	7.38155	.007
		Secondary school	25.01852[a]	7.50039	.008
		High school	22.10256[a]	7.55173	.029
Change O.	Illiterate	Primary school	−.98916	1.10096	.897
		Secondary school	−1.34568	1.60305	.918

(continued)

Table 3.89 (continued)

Dimensions	(I) Educational status of mother	(J) Educational status of mother	Mean difference (I–J)	Std. error	Sig.
		High school	−2.88699	1.77843	.483
		University	−23.93827[a]	6.53133	.002
	Primary school	Illiterate	.98916	1.10096	.897
		Secondary school	−.35652	1.31380	.999
		High school	−1.89783	1.52286	.724
		University	−22.94912[a]	6.46642	.004
	Secondary school	Illiterate	1.34568	1.60305	.918
		Primary school	.35652	1.31380	.999
		High school	−1.54131	1.91749	.929
		University	−22.59259[a]	6.57056	.006
	High school	Illiterate	2.88699	1.77843	.483
		Primary school	1.89783	1.52286	.724
		Secondary school	1.54131	1.91749	.929
		University	−21.05128[a]	6.61553	.013
	University	Illiterate	23.93827[a]	6.53133	.002
		Primary school	22.94912[a]	6.46642	.004
		Secondary school	22.59259[a]	6.57056	.006
		High school	21.05128[a]	6.61553	.013
Communication	Illiterate	Primary school	−4.44690	3.03216	.585
		Secondary school	−5.44444	4.41497	.732
		High school	−9.79487	4.89797	.267
		University	−68.00000[a]	17.98796	.002
	Primary school	Illiterate	4.44690	3.03216	.585
		Secondary school	−.99754	3.61834	.999
		High school	−5.34797	4.19411	.707
		University	−63.55310[a]	17.80919	.004
	Secondary school	Illiterate	5.44444	4.41497	.732
		Primary school	.99754	3.61834	.999
		High school	−4.35043	5.28096	.923
		University	−62.55556[a]	18.09600	.005
	High school	Illiterate	9.79487	4.89797	.267
		Primary school	5.34797	4.19411	.707
		Secondary school	4.35043	5.28096	.923
		University	−58.20513[a]	18.21986	.013
	University	Illiterate	68.00000[a]	17.98796	.002
		Primary school	63.55310[a]	17.80919	.004
		Secondary school	62.55556[a]	18.09600	.005
		High school	58.20513[a]	18.21986	.013

[a]The mean difference is significant at the .05 level

Table 3.90 Kruskal Wallis test results of the difference according to the dimension of educational level of fathers of the employees

Dimensions	Educational status of father	N	Mean
Employee O.	Illiterate	27	282.59
	Primary school	467	310.31
	Secondary school	57	311.78
	High school	62	348.85
	University	15	349.50
	Total	628	
Task O.	Illiterate	27	289.65
	Primary school	467	308.33
	Secondary school	57	3155.55
	High school	62	351.91
	University	15	371.50
	Total	628	
Change O.	Illiterate	27	297.17
	Primary school	467	310.50
	Secondary school	57	306.01
	High school	62	350.82
	University	15	352.23
	Total	628	
Communication D.	Illiterate	27	281.04
	Primary school	467	310.67
	Secondary school	57	317.92
	High school	62	334.75
	University	15	397.40
	Total	628	

	Employee-oriented	Task-oriented	Change-oriented	Communication
Chi-Square	3.894	5.199	3.748	5.060
df	4	4	4	4
Asymp. Sig.	.420	.267	.441	.281

3.10.9 Kruskal Wallis Test Results of the Difference According to the Dimension of Educational Level of Fathers of the Employees

Kruskal Wallis test was performed to determine if there was a difference between leadership behavior sub-dimensions and communication dimension according to educational level of fathers of the employees. Test results are presented in Table 3.90. Since significance levels were found to be smaller than 0.05 according to sub-dimensions of both scales ($p > 0.05$) it was found that there was a significant difference between employee-oriented, task-oriented and change-oriented leadership behavior sub-dimensions and communication sub-dimensions of the employees according to their educational levels. According to this finding, our eleventh hypothesis, H_1 was rejected and hypothesis H_0 was accepted. It was observed that there was a statistically significant difference between educational level of fathers of the employees, leadership behavior types and communication viewpoint of the employees.

Kruskal Wallis and Mann-Whitney U test were performed to determine whether there was a difference between other socio-demographic variables (number of children, working status of the spouse, number of siblings) and leadership behavior sub-dimensions and communication dimension. Since significance levels were found to be greater than 0.05 value ($p > 0.05$), the tables and interpretations about the findings were not deemed necessary to be included in this book.

3.11   Discussion Result and Suggestions

In this part of the study, the relationship between socio-demographic variables of employees working in glass, textile and clothing sectors and leadership behavior type and the communication that employees perceive towards their managers were determined and the findings were interpreted after the discussion was made in parallel with literature information and the results and some suggestions were given.

628 people have attended the study in total 163 of whom are male and 425 of whom are female. 104 of the participants are single while 524 of them are married. 225 of the employees work in glass, 221 of them in textile and 152 of them in clothing sector.

11 hypotheses were developed in the study to be tested and hypotheses 1, 2, 3, 4 and 11 were refused while hypotheses 5, 6, 7, 8, 9 and 10 were accepted. According to the hypothesis 5 which was accepted, a significant difference was found between employees' genders and leadership behavior types and their point of views to communication. The difference of gender in accordance with the accepted hypothesis 5 can be interpreted as a situation which makes different the leadership and point of view to communication.

According to the accepted hypothesis 6, a significant difference was determined between employees' sectors in which they are working and leadership behavior types and point of view towards communication. It can be said that working in different sectors causes employees to perceive leadership manners and communication forms of the managers in different ways.

According to the accepted hypothesis 7, there is a significant difference between employees' family income and leadership behavior types as well as their points of views towards communication. This can be explained as the reason why employees perceive their managers' leadership styles and communication manners differently is the fact that the income levels of employees may be high or low.

According to the accepted hypothesis 8, it was found a significant difference between employees' hometowns where they grew up and leadership behavior types as well as their points of views towards communication. It can be said that employees' hometowns where they grew up (a village or big town) may cause them to perceive managers' leadership styles or communication manners differently.

According to the accepted hypothesis 9, there is a significant difference between employees' educational status and leadership behavior types as well as their points of views towards communication. It can be accepted that educational status of the employees causes them to perceive managers' leadership styles or communication manners differently.

According to the accepted hypothesis 10, there is a significant difference between employees' maternal education status and leadership behavior types as well as their points of views towards communication. It can be said that the educational status of employees' mothers causes them to perceive managers' leadership styles or communication manners differently.

Other five hypotheses were not interpreted due to the fact that they were not accepted and refused. The study reached its aim, because 6 of the 11 hypotheses were accepted which were developed after literature search in line with the purposes of study. It can be said that this study is the first and only in literature due to the fact that it was performed in three sectors whose structures are different. On the other hand, when the content and results of the study is evaluated, it can be said that the study is unique.

Especially, the following results are unique and can be evaluated as a contribution to the literature:

1. Different perceptions of the employees working in different sectors regarding leadership styles and communication skills of their managers,
2. Different perceptions of the employees growing up in different places regarding leadership styles and communication skills of their managers,
3. Different perceptions of the employees possessing different educational status regarding leadership styles and communication skills of their managers,
4. Different perceptions of the employees whose mothers possess different levels of education regarding leadership styles and communication skills of their managers,
5. Different perceptions of the employees possessing different family incomes regarding leadership styles and communication skills of their managers.

Those working in glass sector firstly perceived their managers as worker-oriented, task-oriented and alteration-oriented. According to Kelez's study in which nurses perceive leadership styles of their managers, nurses firstly perceived their managers as task-oriented, worker-oriented and alteration-oriented. As it is seen, while nurses perceive their managers mostly as task-oriented and worker-oriented, employees working in glass sector perceive their managers as worker-oriented and task-oriented. Although these two findings are not consisted; it can be said that our study is consistent with the findings of Kelez's study in terms of alteration. It can be said that differences between the working condition of glass sector and health sector may be shown as the reason of this fact (Kelez 2008:193). According to the study of Tengilimoğlu, it was found that averages of leadership behaviors differ depending on the sector and educational status. This result is consistent with the findings of our study (Tengilimoğlu 2005:38).

It was found that there wasn't a significant difference between genders, ages and seniorities of the employees working in glass, textile and clothing sectors and their points of views towards the communication of their managers. At the same time, according to the study Gürsun carried out with primary school managers, there wasn't any significant difference between genders, ages and seniorities of teachers and their perceived communication skills. Thus, it can be said that the results are consistent. On the other hand, there was a significant difference between educational status of employees working in glass, textile and clothing sectors and their points of views towards their communication of managers. Moreover, similar results were collected in the study performed by Gürsun (2007:133–137). In a study Cesur performed on primary school managers, there was a significant difference between seniorities of teachers at school and communication skills of school managers. This result is not consistent with the results of our study (Cesur 2009:135–137). According to a study performed by Akbaş in banking sector, there wasn't any significant difference between seniority, marital status of employees and their communication levels. This result is consisted with our study. However, while there is a significant difference between educational status of employees working in glass, textile and clothing sectors and their points of views towards the communication of their managers, there wasn't any difference in the study of Akbaş. Therefore, it can be said that there wasn't a consistency (Akbaş 2008:50–56).

Findings of the study which titled Leadership and Organizational Communication: A Study on Glass, Textile and Apparel Sectors were analyzed and evaluated. The results showed that the employees saw friendly the behaviors of their managers; they gave importance and listened to their ideas and suggestions; they trusted them; they did not avoid taking risks while making decisions; they adopted open and honest management; they established good communication with their subordinates; they liked discussing new ideas; they gave importance of obeying rules and principles; they inspired trust and made plans for the future; they gave importance to feedback; they had good communication and dialogue with their subordinates; they gave importance to opinions of their subordinates; they defended their subordinates in various matters; they were open to innovation and change; they were cautious in inspection of work; they created a friendly environment without disputes; they created opportunities to eliminate conflicts; they treated their subordinates fairly; they made quick decisions when necessary; they gave their subordinates the right to speak while making decisions and gave importance to their opinions; they gave clear instructions; they respected their subordinates as individuals; the produced new and different ideas in implementation of works; they analyzed the situations and did not make decisions without thinking and behaved in a cautious manner; they valued motivation; they informed the employees about the results of the work performed; they held periodic meetings with the employees to listen to their problems; they held meetings with the employees to solve the problems; they used written channels of communication to make sure that the subordinates can understand the orders; they adopted and implemented open door policy; they established relaxed communication with the employees; they spared enough time to listen to the employees and they valued them; they informed the employees about the situation in the work place and gave importance to the employees; they appreciated good work; they gave importance to establishing accurate and effective communication to avoid making mistakes at work; they used all means of communication; they were respected by the employees for their behaviors and personality traits; they respected the opinions and suggestions of employees; they checked whether the subordinates fully understood their orders by asking them questions; they used clear; simple and understandable sentences while speaking to subordinates; they communicated by considering the situation and conditions of the employees, they used body language very well while speaking; they had good time management; they made eye contact with the employees while speaking to them; they criticized the employees without hurting or demotivating the employees; they did not interrupt the employees unless necessary and they listened to them; they did not criticize or say anything negative to the employees in a community.

Last of all, there was no significant difference between marital status of the employees and leadership behavior types and communication viewpoints;

There was no significant difference between working status of the spouses of the employees and leadership behavior types and communication viewpoints;

There was no significant difference between age groups of the employees and leadership behavior types and communication viewpoints;

There was no significant difference between education levels of fathers of the employees and leadership behavior types and communication viewpoints;

There was no significant difference between seniority levels the employees and leadership behavior types and communication viewpoints.

As a result of this present study, there was a significant difference between gender of the employees and leadership behavior types and communication viewpoints. When compared to female employees, male employees were found to consider leadership behaviors and communication process of their leaders more positively. Male employees consider their managers as more employee-oriented, task-oriented and change-oriented than female employees. It was observed that male employees had a different perception of communication dimension of their managers when compared to female employees. As a result, it was found that gender of the employees created different perceptions of leadership behavior and communication process.

As a result, there was a significant difference between employee-oriented, task-oriented and change-oriented leadership behaviors sub-dimensions and working sectors of the employees. It was found that when compared to the employees working in textile sector, the employees in glass sector considered their managers as more employee-oriented leaders. Similarly, when compared to the employees working in textile sector, the employees working in glass sector considered their managers more task-oriented and when compared to the employees working in textile sector, the employees working in apparel sector found their managers as more task-oriented.

The results of the study showed that when compared to the employees in textile sector, the employees in glass sector found their managers as more change-oriented. When compared to the employees in textile sector, the employees in apparel sector found their managers as more change-oriented. On the other hand, when compared to the employees in textile sector, the employee working in glass sector found their managers as more successful in communication process. When compared to the employees in textile sector, the employees in apparel sector found their managers as more successful in communication process. It was found that there was a significant difference between employee-oriented, task-oriented and change-oriented leadership behavior sub-dimensions and communication dimension according to the working sectors of the employees. Based on this finding, it was observed that the employees working in different sectors had different perceptions of leadership behaviors. In addition, it was found that the employees working in different sectors had different perceptions about their leaders' communication process.

The results showed that when compared to the employees who grew up in villages or cities, the employees who grew up in large cities perceived their managers as task-oriented leaders. Similarly, when compared to the employees who grew up in villages or cities, the employees who grew up in districts found their managers as task-oriented. On the other hand, when compared to the employees who grew up in villages, the employee who grew up in large cities found their managers more successful in communication. In other words, the employees who grew up in large cities considered their leaders as the ones who can establish very good communication with them. On the other hand, it was found that the employees who grew up in large cities perceived their managers as task and change-oriented leaders. Thus, it was concluded that the employees had different perceptions of leadership behaviors and communication processes according to their residing place and place of upbringing.

As a result of this study, there was a significant difference between employee-oriented, task-oriented and change-oriented leadership behavior sub-dimensions and communication dimension according to income levels of the employees. When compared to the employees in 700 TL and below income group, the employees in 2,201–3,700 TL income group perceived their managers as more employee-oriented leaders. Similarly, it was found that when compared to the employees in 700 TL and below income group and 701–2,200 TL income group, the employees in 2,201–3,700 TL income group perceived their managers as more task-oriented leaders. When compared to the employees in 700 TL and below income group and 701–2,200 TL income group, the employees in 2,201–3,700 TL income group perceived their managers as more change-oriented leaders. In terms of communication scale, it was found that the employees in 700 TL and below income group, the employees in 2,201–3,700 TL income group perceived their managers as more successful in communication process. According to these findings income levels of the employees caused different perceptions of leadership behavior and communication process.

It was found that there was a significant difference between employee-oriented, task-oriented and change-oriented leadership behavior sub-dimensions and communication dimension according to educational levels of the employees. Employees with 2-year degree were found to consider their leaders as employee-oriented leaders when compared to employees who were primary school, secondary school and high school graduates. Similarly, when compared to primary school graduates, high school graduates perceived their managers as employee-oriented. It was found that, when compared to primary school, secondary school and high school graduates, the employees with 2-year degree perceived their leaders as task-oriented leaders. Similarly, when compared to primary school graduates, high school graduates perceived their leaders as task-oriented leaders. It was found that when compared to primary school, secondary school and high school graduates, the employees with 2-year degree perceived their managers as change-oriented leaders. On the other hand, when compared to primary school, secondary school and high school graduates, the employees with 2-year degree found their managers as more effective in communication process. Thus, it was concluded that educational level of the employees affected the perceptions of the employees in terms of leadership behaviors and communication process.

As a result, there was a significant difference between employee-oriented, task-oriented and change-oriented leadership behavior sub-dimensions and communication dimension. The employees whose mothers were university graduates were found to perceive their managers as employee-oriented when compared to the employees whose mothers were illiterate. It was found that the employees whose mothers were university graduates perceived their managers as task-oriented when compared to the employees whose mothers were illiterate, primary school, secondary school and high school graduates. When compared to the employees whose mothers were illiterate, primary school, secondary school or high school graduates, the employees whose mothers were university graduates perceived their managers as change-oriented leaders. On the other hand, it was found that the employees whose mothers were university graduates found their managers more successful in communication process when compared to the employees whose mothers were illiterate, primary school, secondary school or high school graduates. It was concluded that educational level of the mothers of the employees was a factor which caused different perceptions of leadership behavior and communication process.

Last of all, there was no significant difference between employee-oriented, task-oriented and change-oriented leadership behavior sub-dimensions and communication dimension according to educational level of fathers of the employees.

We suggest that future studies on leadership should handle this subject in combination with a different subject of organizational behavior. Furthermore, the present study can be applied in other sectors and existing situation about leadership behaviors can be investigated.

References

Aamodt, Michael G. (2010). *Industrial/Organizational Psychology, Ann Applied Approach,* Wadsworth Cengage Learning, Sixth Edition, USA.

Acar, Füsun. (2002). Duygusal Zeka ve Liderlik, *Erciyes Üniversitesi Sosyal Bilimler Enstitüsü Dergisi,* Sayı.12, 53-68.

Ada, Nesrin, Alver İpek ve Atlı Fatma. (2008). "Örgütsel İletişimin Örgütsel Bağlılık Üzerine Etkisi: Manisa Organize Sanayi Bölgesinde Yer alan ve İmalat Sektörü Çalışanları Üzerinde Yapılan Bir Araştırma", *Ege Akademik Bakış Dergisi,* 8, (2), 487-518.

Adair, John. (2004). *Etkili İletişim,* Çeviren: Ömer Çevikoğlu, Babıali Kültür Yayıncılığı, 2. Baskı, İstanbul.

Akbaş, Bahadır. (2008). "Örgütsel İletişimin Örgütsel Bağlılığa Etkisi Üzerine Bir Araştırma" Afyon Kocatepe Üniversitesi Sosyal Bilimler Enstitüsü, Yayınlanmamış Yüksek Lisans Tezi.

Akdemir, Ali. (2008). *Vizyon Yönetimi,* Ekin Basın Yayın Dağıtım, Bursa.

Akıncı, Z.Beril. (1998). *Kurum Kültürü ve Örgütsel İletişim,*İletişim Yayınları Cep Üniversitesi, İstanbul.

Akyurt, Nuran. (2009). "Sağlıkta İletişim ve Marmara Üniversitesi Sağlık Hizmetleri Meslek Yüksekokulu Öğrencilerinin İletişim Becerileri" *Fırat Sağlık Hizmetleri Dergisi,*Cilt:4, Sayı:11, 15-33.

Ambrose, Delorese, (1991). *Leadership,* Third Edition, Kendall/Hunt Publishing, USA.

Anadolu Üniversitesi Psikolojik Danışma ve Rehberlik Merkezi, *Beden Dili, http://www.pdrm. anadolu.edu.tr/b/bedendili.pdf.* Accessed 18.11.2011

Aksel, İbrahim, v.d., (2008). *Liderlik ve Motivasyon Geleneksel ve Güncel Yaklaşımlar,* Editör: Celalettin Serinkan. Nobel Yayın Dağıtım, Ankara.

Aksu, Ali. (2009). "Kriz Yönetimi ve Vizyoner Liderlik", *Journal Of Yaşar University,* No:15, Vol:4, Temmuz Sayısı, 2435-2450

Altun, Sadegül Akbaba. (2003). "İlköğretim Okulu Müdürlerinin Dönüşümcü Liderliğe Verdikleri Önem ve Uygulama Düzeyleri", *İlköğretim Online Dergisi,* Vol:2, Sayı:1, 10-17. http://www.ilköğretim-online.org.tr

Arısoy, Burcu. (2007). "Örgütsel İletişimin Motivasyon ve İş Doyumu Üzerine Etkileri", *Marmara Üniversitesi Sosyal Bilimler Enstitüsü,* Yayınlanmamış Yüksek Lisans Tezi, İstanbul.

Arslan, Aykut. (2009). "Kriz Yönetiminde Liderlik", *Akademik Bakış Uluslararası Hakemli Sosyal Bilimler E-Dergisi,* Sayı: 18, 1-12. http://www.akademikbakis.org/18/12lider.pdf.

Arslan, F.Müge ve Bayçu, Sevil. (2006). *Mağaza Atmosferi,* Editör:Mine Oyman, Anadolu Üniversitesi Yayınları, Eskişehir.

S. Ünsar, *Leadership and Communication,* Contributions to Management Science, 125
DOI 10.1007/978-3-319-05248-9, © Springer International Publishing Switzerland 2014

Arslantaş, C. Cüneyt ve Dursun, Meral. (2008). "Etik Liderlik Davranışının Yöneticiye Duyulan Güven ve Psikolojik Güçlendirme Üzerindeki Etkisinde Etkileşim Adaletinin Dolaylı Rolü" *Anadolu Üniversitesi Sosyal Bilimler Dergisi,* Cilt:8, Sayı:1, 111-128.

Asunakutlu, Tuncer. (2001). "Klasik ve Neo-Klasik Dönemde Örgütsel Güvenin Karşılaştırılması Üzerine Bir Deneme" Muğla Üniversitesi SBE Dergisi, Bahar, Sayı:5, 1-17.

Atak. Metin. (2005). "Örgütlerde Resmi Olmayan İletişimin Yeri ve Önemi" *Havacılık ve Uzay Teknolojileri Dergisi,* Cilt:2, Sayı:2, 59-67.

Atar, Emrah ve Özbek, Oğuz. (2009). "Beden Eğitimi Ve Spor Yüksekokulu Öğrencilerinin Liderlik Davranışları", *Spormetre Beden Eğitimi ve Spor Bilimleri Dergisi,* VII (2), 51-59.

Avcı, Gürkan. (2009). "Ankara İli Mamak İlçesi Kamu Eğitim Kurumları Yöneticilerinin Belge Yönetiminde Yaşadıkları Sorunlar Ve Çözüm Önerileri" Ankara Üniversitesi Eğitim Bilimleri Enstitüsü, Yayınlanmamış Yüksek Lisans Tezi, Ankara.

Avcı, Umut ve Topaloğlu, Cafer. (2009). " Hiyerarşik Kademelere Göre Liderlik Davranışlarını Algılama Farklılıkları: Otel Çalışanları Üzerinde Bir Araştırma", *Karamanoğlu Mehmet Bey Üniversitesi İİBF Sosyal ve Ekonomik Araştırmalar Dergisi,*Yıl:11, Sayı:16, 1-20.

Aykan, Ebru. (2004). "Kayseri'de Faaliyet Gösteren Girişimcilerin Liderlik Özellikleri", *Erciyes Üniversitesi Sosyal Bilimler Enstitü Dergisi,* Sayı:17, 213-224.

Bakan, İsmail. (2008). "Örgüt Kültürü" ve "Liderlik" Türlerine İlişkin Algılamalar ile Yöneticilerin Demografik Özellikleri Arasındaki İlişki: Bir Alan Araştırması" *Karamanoğlu Mehmet Bey Üniversitesi Sosyal ve Ekonomik Araştırmalar İİBF Dergisi,* Yıl:10, Sayı:14, Haziran Sayısı, 13-40.

Bakan, İsmail ve Büyükbeşe, Tuba. (2010). " Liderlik Türleri ve Güç Kaynakları'na İlişkin Mevcut- Gelecek Durum Karşılaştırması: Eğitim Kurumu Yöneticilerinin Algılarına Dayalı Bir Alan Araştırması", " *Karamanoğlu Mehmet Bey Üniversitesi Sosyal ve Ekonomik Araştırmalar İİBF Dergisi,* Yıl:12, Sayı:19, Aralık Sayısı, 73-84.

Baloğlu, Nuri ve Karadağ, Engin. (2009). "Ruhsal Liderlik Üzerine Teorik Bir Çözümleme", *Kuram ve Uygulamada Eğitim Yönetimi,* Cilt 15, Sayı 58, 165-190.

Baltaş, Acar. (2001). *Ekip Çalışması ve Liderlik,* Remzi Kitabevi, Üçüncü Baskı, İstanbul.

Baltaş, Acar. (2010). *Türk Kültüründe Yönetmek, Yerel Değerlerle Küresel Başarılar Kazanmak,* Remzi Kitabevi, İstanbul.

Baransel, Atilla. (1993). *Çağdaş Yönetim Düşüncesinin Evrimi,* İstanbul Üniversitesi İşletme Fakültesi Yayını, Cilt 1, 3.Baskı, İstanbul.

Barker, Lary L. (1990). *Communication,* Prentice Hall, Fifth Edition, USA.

Barkan, Murat ve Eroğlu, Erhan. (2004). "Eğitim İletişiminde Çağdaş Ortamlar: ".. İletişim Bir Sorun Kaynağı mı Yoksa Çözüm Seçeneği mi?.." *The Turkish Online Journal of Educational Technology – TOJET,* July, Volume: 3, Issue 3, http://www.tojet.net/articles/3314.pdf, 115-123.

Barut Yaşar, Gökalp Murat, Akdenk Mursel, Kalafat Mursel ve Menteşe Sabit (2010). "The Associations Between University Students' Transformational Leadership Characteristics And Dysfunctional Limitedness Perceptions", *Procedia Social and Behavioral Sciences,* Vol: 9 132-136.

Barutçugil, İsmet. (2004). *Stratejik İnsan Kaynakları Yönetimi,* Kariyer Yayıncılık İletişim, Eğitim Hiz. Ltd.Şti. İstanbul.

Bass, Bernard M. (1998). *Tranformational Leadership,* Lawrence Erlbaum Associates, Inc., USA.

Başaran, İbrahim Ethem. (2000). *Yönetim,* Bilim Kitap ve Umut Yayım Dağıtım, Feryal Matbaası, 3. Baskı, Ankara.

Başaran, İbrahim Ethem. (2004). *Yönetimde İnsan İlişkileri Yönetsel Davranış,* Nobel Yayın Dağıtım, 3. Baskı, Ankara.

Baysal, A.Can ve Tekarslan, Erdal. (1998). *Davranış Bilimleri,* İstanbul Üniversitesi İşletme Fakültesi Yayını, İstanbul.

Bender, Peter Urs. (2000). *İçten Liderlik,* Türkçesi: İ.Kalyoncu, F.C.Akbaş, Hayat Yayınları, İstanbul.

Benligiray, Serap. (2005). *Büro Yönetimi,* Anadolu Üniversitesi Yayınları, Eskişehir.

Berger, Arthur Asa. (1995). *Essentials of Mass Communicatin Theory,* Sage Publications, Inc. USA.

Bettinghaus, Erwin P. (2004). *Research, Principles, and Practices in Visual Communication, (Communication Models),* Information Age Publishing Inc. USA.

Bhardwaj, Rajul ve Madan Pankai. (2009). *Rol Models in Management (Leadeship and Communication),* Global Vision Publishing House, India.

Bıçakçı, İlker. (1998). *İletişim ve Halkla İlişkiler Eleştirel Bir Yaklaşım,* Media Cat Yayınları, Ankara.

Bilgin, Leman, Taşçı Deniz, Kağnıcıoğlu Deniz, Benligiray Serap, Tonus, H.Zümrüt. (2004). *İnsan Kaynakları Yönetimi,* Editör: Ramazan Geylan, Anadolu Üniversitesi Yayınları, Eskişehir.

Bingham, Jane, Chandler Fiona, Chisholm Jane, Harvey Gilli Miles Lisa, Reid Struan ve Taplin Sam. (2010). *Antik Dünya Ansiklopedisi,* Tübitak Popüler Bilim Kitapları, 1. Basım, Ankara.

Bolat, Tamer ve Seymen, Aytemiz. (2003). "Örgütlerde İş Etiğinin Yerleştirilmesinde "Dönüşümcü Liderlik Tarzı"nın Etkileri Üzerine Bir Değerlendirme", *Balıkesir Sosyal Bilimler Enstitüsü Dergisi,* Cilt.6, Sayı:9, 59-85.

Bordenave, Juan Diaz. (2006). *Communication For Social Change Anthology: Historical and Contemporary Readings,* Edited by, Alfanso Gumucio-Dagro and Thomas Tufte, Communication For Social Change Consortium Inc. New Jersey, USA.

Budak, Gülay ve Budak, Gönül. (2004). *İşletme Yönetimi,* Barış Yayınları Fakülteler Kitabevi, 5. Bası, İzmir.

Budak, Gülay ve Budak, Gönül . (2010a). *İşletme Yönetimi,* Barış Yayınları, Fakülteler Kitabevi, 6. Baskı, İzmir.

Budak, Gönül ve Budak, Gülay. (2010b). *İmaj Mühendisliği Vizyonundan Halkla İlişkiler,* Barış Yayınları, Fakülteler Kitabevi, 5. Bası, İzmir.

Bulut, Yakup ve Uygun, Serdar Vural. (2010). "Etkin Bir Yönetim İçin Vizyoner Liderliğin Önemi: Hatay'daki Kamu Kurumları Üzerinde Bir Uygulama" *Mustafa Kemal Üniversitesi Sosyal Bilimler Enstitüsü Dergisi, Cilt:* 7, Sayı: 13, 29–47.

Can, Halil, Tuncer, Doğan ve Ayhan, Doğan Yaşar. (1999). *Genel İşletmecilik Bilgileri,* Siyasal Kitabevi, Ankara.

Certo, Samuel C. (2003). *Modern Management,* Prentice Hall, Ninth Edition, USA.

Cesur, Hüsnü. (2009). "Ortaöğretim Müdürlerinin Liderlik Stilleri ve İletişim Becerileri Arasındaki İlişkinin Öğretmen Algılarına Göre Değerlendirilmesi (Şişli İlçesi Örneği)", Yeditepe Üniversitesi Sosyal Bilimler Enstitüsü, Yayınlanmamış Yüksek Lisans Tezi.

Choi, Sanghan. (2007). "Democratic Leadership: The Lessons of Exemplary Models for Democratic Governance" *International Journal of Leadership Studies,* Vol: 2, Issue: 3, 243-262.

Cüceloğlu, Doğan. (1992). *Yeniden İnsan İnsana,* Remzi Kitabevi, 2.Basım, İstanbul.

Cüceloğlu, Doğan. (2002). *Keşkesiz Bir Yaşam İçin İletişim Donanımları* Remzi Kitabevi, 9. Basım, İstanbul.

Çağırcı, Simge ve Yeğenoğlu, Selen. (2007). "Genel İletişim Bilgileri Perspektifinden Hasta-Eczacı İletişimi", *Ankara Eczacılık Fakültesi Dergisi,* 36 (1), 31-46.

Çakar, Ulaş ve Arbak, Yasemin. (2003). "Dönüşümcü Liderlik Duygusal Zekâ Gerektirir Mi? Yöneticiler Üzerinde Örnek Bir Çalışma" *Dokuz Eylül Ü.İ.İ.B.F.Dergisi Cilt:18 Sayı:2, 83- 98.*

Çalışkan, Behlül. (2009). "Enformasyonun Metalaşması Üzerine", *Marmara İletişim Dergisi,* Temmuz, Sayı:15, 23-46.

Çetin, Nesrin Gökben ve Beceren, Ertan. (2007). "Lider Kişilik: Gandhi", *Süleyman Demirel Üniversitesi Sosyal Bilimler Enstitüsü Dergisi,* Yıl:3, Sayı/: 5, 110-132.

Çeyiz, Senem. (2007). "Adana İlinde Futbol Antrenörlüğü Yapan Bireylerin Liderlik Tarzlarının Belirlenmesi", Çukurova Üniversitesi Sağlık Bilimleri Enstitüsü, Yayınlanmamış Yüksek Lisans Tezi.

Çoban, Onur. Laswell Modeli, http://www.onurcoban.com/2011/09/lasswell-modeli.html), Accessed 03.11.2011

Daft, Richard L. (1991). *Management,* The Dreyden Press, Second Edition, USA.

Daft, Richard L. ve Marcic, Dorothy. (2006). *Understanding Management*, Thomson South-Western, Fifth Edition, USA.

Daft, Richard L. (2008). *The Leadeship Experince*, Thomson South-Western Corporation, Fourth Edition, USA.

Daft, Richard L. (2008). *Management*, Thomson South-Western Corporation, Eighth Edition, USA.

Davis, Keith. (1984). *İşletmelerde İnsan Davranışı*, İstanbul Üniversitesi İşletme Fakültesi Yayını, Çevirenler: K.Tosun,T.Somay,F.Aykar,C.Baysal,Ö.Sadullah, S.Yalçın. İstanbul.

Deryakulu, Deniz. (1992). "Eğitim İletişimi Kavramı", *Ankara Üniversitesi Eğitim Bilimleri Fakültesi Dergisi*, Cilt: 25 Sayı: 2, 787-794.

Dessler, Gary. (1998). *Management*, Prentice-Hall International, Inc. International Edition. USA.

Doğan, Selen ve Kılıç, Selçuk. (2009). "Bilgi Yönetiminde Liderliğin Rolü Üzerine Kavramsal Bir İnceleme", *Süleyman Demirel Üniversitesi İktisadi ve İdari BilimlerFakültesi Dergisi*, Cilt:14, Sayı:2. 87-111.

Doğanalp, Burcu. (2009). "Kriz Döneminde Transformasyonel Lider Davranışlarının İşletme Performansı Bağlamında Fırsat Yönetimine Etkisi: Bankacılık Sektöründe Bir Uygulama", *Selçuk Üniversitesi Sosyal Bilimler Enstitüsü Dergisi*, Sayı:22, 131-146.

Drake, Richard İ. ve Smith, Peter J. (1990). *Sanayide Davranış Bilimleri*, İstanbul Üniversitesi İşletme Fakültesi Yayını, Çevirenler: K.Tosun, İ.Erdoğan, F.Aykar, T.Somay, A., M. Ergündüz, İstanbul.

DuBrin, Andrew J. (2012). *Essentials Of Management*, Ninth Edition, South-Western Cengage Learning, USA.

DuBrin, Andrew J. (2010). *Leadership, Research Findings, Practice, and Skills*, South-Western Cengage Learning, Sixth Edition, USA.

Durukan, Erdil, Can, Süleyman, Arıkan, A.Naci ve Göktaş Zekeriya. (2006). "Selçuk Üniversitesi Beden Eğitimi Ve Spor Yüksekokulu Öğrencilerinin Yapıyı Kurma Boyutunda Liderlik Davranışlarının Sınıf Düzeylerine Göre Karşılaştırılması", *Balıkesir Üniversitesi Sosyal Bilimler Enstitüsü Dergisi*, Cilt:9, Sayı:15, 1-19.

Durukan, Haydar. (2006). "Okul Yöneticisinin Vizyoner Liderlik Rolü" *Ahi Evran Üniversitesi Kırşehir Eğitim Fakültesi Dergisi*, Cilt 7, Sayı 2, 277-286.

Efil, İsmail. (2010). *İşletmelerde Yönetim ve Organizasyon*, Dora Basım Yayım Dağıtım Ltd. Şti, 11. Baskı, Bursa.

Ekvall, G. ve Arvonen, J. (1991), " Change –centred Leadership: An Extension of the Two Dimensional Model", Scandinavian Journal of Management, Volume 7, pp.17-26.

Elgünler, Tuğçe Çedikçi ve Fener, Tuğba Çedikçi. (2011). "İletişimin Kalitesini Etkileyen Engeller ve Bu Engellerin Giderilmesi" *The Turkish Online Journal of Design, Art and Communication – TOJDAC July* , Vol:1 Issue 1, 35-39.

Erbaydar, Tuğrul. (2003). "Halk Sağlığı Açısından Sağlık İletişimi" *Cumhuriyet Üniversitesi Tıp Fakültesi Dergisi*, 25(4), özel ek, 45-51.

Eren, Erol, (2007). *Örgütsel Davranış ve Yönetim Psikolojisi*, Beta Basım Yayım Dağıtım A.Ş., 10. Baskı, İstanbul.

Eren, Erol, (2003). *Yönetim ve Organizasyon (Çağdaş ve Küresel Yaklaşımlar)*, Beta Basım Yayım Dağıtım A.Ş., 6. Bası, İstanbul.

Eren, Erol. (1993). *Yönetim Psikolojisi*, Beta Basım Yayım Dağıtım A.Ş., İstanbul.

Erdoğan, İlhan. (1997). *İşletmelerde Davranış*, İstanbul Üniversitesi İşletme Fakültesi Yayınları, 2. Bası, İstanbul.

Ergeneli, Azize. (2006). *Örgüt ve İnsan*, Hacettepe Üniversitesi Yayınları, Ankara.

Erkuş, Ahmet ve Günlü, Ebru. (2009). "İletişim Tarzının ve Sözsüz İletişim Düzeyinin Çalışanların İş Performansına Etkisi: Beş Yıldızlı Otel İşletmelerinde Bir Araştırma", *Anatolia: Turizm Araştırmaları Dergisi*, Cilt: 20, Sayı:1, 7-24.

Eroğlu, Erhan ve Sunel, Gürler. (2003). "Yöneticilerin iletişim Becerilerinin Değerlendirilmesi ve Penguen Gıda İşletmesinde bir Uygulama" *Review of Social, Economic & Business Studies*, Vol.3/4, 178-203.

Ertürk, Mümin. (2009a). *İşletmelerde Yönetim ve Organizasyon*, Beta Basım Yayım Dağıtım, 4. Baskı, İstanbul.

Ertürk, Mümin. (2009b). *İşletme Biliminin Temel İlkeleri*, Beta Basım Yayım Dağıtım, 7. Baskı, İstanbul.

Fiske, John. (1990). *Introduction To Comunication Studies*, 2nd Edition, Routledge, New York.

Fourie, Pieter J. (2007). *Media Studies*, Volume One, Institutions, Theories and Issues, Juta Edition, South Africa.

Freeman, Allyn. (2008). *Liderlik Dehası ve Alfred Sloan*, Çeviren: M.F.İmre, Türkiye İş Bankası Kültür Yayınları, İstanbul.

Friedman, George. (2009). *Gelecek 100 Yıl 21. Yüzyıl İçin Öngörüler*, Çevirenler: İbrahim Şener, Enver Günsel, Pegasus Yayınları, İstanbul.

Fry Louis W., T, Vitucci Steve, Cedillo Marie. (2005). "Spiritual Leadership And Army Transformation: Theory, Measurement, And Establishing a Baseline" *The Leadership Quarterly*, Volume:16, Issue: 5, 835-862.

Fry Louis ve Slocum Jr. (2008). "Maximizing the Triple Bottom Line through Spiritual Leadership", *Organizational Dynamics*, Vol. 37, No. 1, pp. 86–96.

George, Jennifer M. and Jones, Gareth R. (2012). *Understanding and Managing Organizational Behavior*, Sixth Edition, Prentice Hall, USA.

George, William. (2003). *Authentic Leadership*, Jossey Bass A Wiley Imprint, USA.

Gerson, Mark. (2006). *Çatışmalı Ortamlarda Liderlik*, Çeviren: Ahmet Kardam, Mess Yayınları, İstanbul.

Gillet, Joris, Cartwright, Edward ve Vugt, Mark Van. (2011). "Selfish Or Servant Leadership? Evolutionary Predictions On Leadership Personalities In Koordination Games" *Personality and Individual Differences*, (51), 231–236.

Gökçe, Orhan. (2002). *İletişim Bilimine Giriş*, Turhan Kitabevi, 4, Basım, Ankara.

Gönülşen, Ömür ve Sevim, Leyla. (2005). "Reddin' in Üç Boyutlu Liderlik Teorisi'nin Liderlik Literatüründeki Yerinin İrdelenmesi ve Ampirik Bir Araştırma" *Celal Bayar Üniversitesi Yönetim ve Ekonomi Dergisi*, Cilt:12, Sayı:2, 91-103.

Güney, Salih. v.d. (2007a). *Yönetim ve Organizasyon, (Yönetim ve Organizasyonun Bazı Temel Kavramları Bölümü)*, Editör: Salih Güney, Nobel Yayın Dağıtım, 2. Baskı, Ankara

Güney, Salih. v.d. (2007b). *Yönetim ve Organizasyon, (Bireylerarası İletişim Bölümü)*, Editör: Salih Güney, Nobel Yayın Dağıtım, 2. Baskı, Ankara

Güney, Semra. et al., (2007). *Yönetim ve Organizasyon, (Liderlik Bölümü)*, Editör: Salih Güney, Nobel Yayın Dağıtım, 2. Baskı, Ankara

Gürgen, Haluk, Kırel Çiğdem, Uztuğ Ferruh, Orhon, Nezih. (2005). *Halkla İlişkiler ve İletişim*, Editör: Ferruf Uztuğ, Anadolu Üniversitesi Yayını, Eskişehir.

Gürsel, Musa, Izgar, Hüseyin, Altınok Vicdan, Kesici Şahin, Bozgeyikli Hasan, Sürücü Abdullah ve Nehiş Ayşe. (2003). *Endüstri ve Örgüt Psikolojisi*, Eğitim Kitabevi Yayınları, Konya.

Gürsun, Yasemin. (2007). " İlköğretim Okulu Müdürlerinin Öğretmenler Tarafından Algılanan Öğretimsel Liderlik Rolleri ile İletişim Tarzları Arasındaki İlişkinin İncelenmesi (Kartal İlçesi Örneği), Yeditepe Üniversitesi Sosyal Bilimler Enstitüsü, Yayınlanmamış Yüksek Lisans Tezi

Hacıoğlu, Burcu. (2007). "Duygusal Zekanın Örgütsel İletişim Üzerindeki Etkileri ve Bir Araştırma" Kadir Has Üniversitesi Sosyal Bilimler Enstitüsü, Yayınlanmamış Yüksek Lisans Tezi.

Hogg Michael A. and Vaughan Graham M. (2007). *Sosyal Psikoloji*, Ütopya Yayınevi, Çevirenler: İbrahim Yıldız ve Aydın Gelmez, Ankara.

Hamilton, Cheryl. (2011). *Communicating for Results: A Guide for Business and the Professions*, Ninth Edition, Wadsworth, USA.

İbicioğlu, Hasan, Özmen, İbrahim ve Taş, Sebahattin. (2009). "Liderlik Davranışı ve Toplumsal Norm İlişkisi", *Süleyman Demirel Üniversitesi İİBF Dergisi*, Cilt:14, Sayı:2, 1-23.

İnce, Nedim. (2006). "Farklı Yelken Sınıflarındaki Sporcuların Liderlik Tercihleri" Mersin Üniversitesi Sağlık Bilimleri Enstitüsü, Yayınlanmamış Yüksek Lisans Tezi.

İnce, Mehmet, Bedük, Aykut ve Aydoğan, Enver. (2004). " Örgütlerde Takım Çalışmasına Yönelik Etkin Liderlik Nitelikleri", *Selçuk Üniversitesi Sosyal Bilimler Enstitüsü Dergisi*, Sayı:11, 423-446

Kan, Melanie M. ve Parry, Ken W. (2004). " Identifying Paradox: A Grounded Theory of Leadership İn Overcoming Resistance To Change" *The Leadership Quarterly*, Volume:15, Issue: 4, 467-491.

Karahan, Atilla. (2009). "Bilgi Liderliğinin Verimlilik Üzerine Etkisi: Sağlık Sektöründe Bir Araştırma" *Bilgi Dünyası*, 10 (1), 60-79.

Karalar, Serol. (2010). "Yöneticilerde Demografik Özelliklerin Liderlik İçin Yeterliliği: İstanbul'daki Beş Yıldızlı Oteller Üzerinde Bir Araştırma", Trakya Üniversitesi Sosyal Bilimler Enstitüsü, Yayınlanmamış Yüksek Lisans Tezi.

Karalar, Rıdvan, Benligiray Serap, Coşkun Metin, Oyman Mine, Ulukan, Cemil. (2006). *Perakende Mağaza Yönetimi*, Editör: Gülfidan Barış, Anadolu Üniversitesi Yayını, Eskişehir.

Kasım, Metin. (2009). "Spiker Olmak O Kadar Kolay mı?" *Selçuk Üniversitesi Türkiyat Araştırmaları Dergisi*, Sayı:25, Bahar Sayısı, 209-228.

Kaya, Bayram. (2003). *Bütünleşik Kurumsal İletişim*, Siyasal Kitabevi, Ankara.

Kaynak, Tuğray. (1990). *Organizasyonel Davranış*, İstanbul Üniversitesi İşletme Fakültesi Yayını, İstanbul.

Kaynak, Tuğray, Adal Zeki, Ataay İsmail, Uyargil Cavide, Sadullah Ömer, Acar Ahmet Cevat, Özçelik Oya, Dündar Gönen ve Uluhan Reha. (1998). *İnsan Kaynakları Yönetimi*, İstanbul Üniversitesi İşletme Fakültesi Yayını, İstanbul.

Kelez, Aycan. (2008). "Hemşirelerin Örgüt Kültürünü ve Yöneticilerinin Liderlik Davranışını Algılamaları", Marmara Üniversitesi Sağlık Bilimleri Enstitüsü, Yayınlanmamış Yüksek Lisans Tezi.

Kesken, Jülide ve Ayyıldız, Nazlı Ayşe. (2008). "Liderlik Yaklaşımlarında Yeni Perspektifler: Pozitif ve Otantik Liderlik", *Ege Akademik Bakış Dergisi*, 8(2), 729-754.

Kırel, Çiğdem, Kayaoğlu, Aysel ve Gökdağ Rüçhan. (2004). *Sosyal Psikoloji*, Editör: Sezen Ünlü, Anadolu Üniversitesi Yayını, 1..Baskı, Eskişehir.

Koçel, Tamer, (2005). *İşletme Yöneticiliği*, Arıkan BasımYayım Dağıtım Ltd.Şti., 10 Bası, İstanbul.

Koçel, Tamer, (2010). *İşletme Yöneticiliği*, Beta Basım Yayım Dağıttım A.Ş., 12. Baskı, İstanbul.

Kolasa, Blair J, (1979). *İşletmeler İçin Davranış Bilimlerine Giriş*, İstanbul Üniversitesi İşletme Fakültesi İşletme İktisadı Enstitüsü Yayını, Çevirenler: K.Tosun, F.Aykar, T.Somay, M. Menteşe, İstanbul.

Kongar, Emre. (1983). *Devrim Tarihi ve Toplum Bilimi Açısından Atatürk*, Remzi Kitabevi, 1. Basım, İstanbul.

Kozlu, Cem. (2009). *Liderin Takım Çantası Araçlar ve Yaklaşımlar*, Remzi Kitabevi, 6.Basım, İstanbul.

Köksal, Onur. (2011). "Bir Kültürel Liderlik Paradoksu: Paternalizm", *Mustafa Kemal Üniversitesi Sosyal Bilimler Enstitüsü Dergisi*, Cilt: 8, Sayı: 15, 101 - 122

Liden, Robert, C., Wayne, Sandy, J., Zhao, Hao ve Henderson, David. (2008)."Servant leadership: Development of a Multidimensional Measure and Multi-Level Assessment" *The Leadership Quarterly*, Volume:19, Issue:2, 161-177.

Lussier, Robert N. Ve Achua, Christopher F. (2010). *Leadership Theory, Application, and Skill Development*, Fourth Edition, South Western Cengage Learning, USA.

Maciariello, Joseph A. (2005). *Gün Gün Drucker*, Çeviren: Murat Çetinbakış, Mess Yayınları, İstanbul.

Marquis, Bessie L. And Huston, Carol J. (2009). *Leadership Roles and Management Function in Nursing Theory and Application*, Wolters Kluvwer Health/Lippincott Williams&Wilkins USA, 6th Edition.

Maxwell, John C. (1999a). *Liderlik Nitelikleri*, Türkçesi: İbrahim Şener, Beyaz Yayınları, İstanbul.

Maxwell, John C. (1999b). *Liderlik Yasaları*, Türkçesi: İbrahim Şener, Beyaz Yayınları, İstanbul.

McKeown, Neil. (2005). *Case Studies and Projects in Communication*, Taylor and Francis e-Libraray, U.K.

McNeill, William H. (2008). *Dünya Tarihi*, Çeviren: Alaeddin Şenel, 13. Baskı, İmge Kitabevi, Ankara.

Megep. (2007). (Meslekî Eğitim ve Öğretim Sisteminin Güçlendirilmesi Projesi), İş Hayatında İletişim, Milli Eğitim Bakanlığı, Ankara, http://cygm.meb.gov.tr/modulerprogramlar/kursprogramlari/meslekigelisim/moduller/is_hayatinda_iletisim.pdf Accessed.15.07.2013

Megep II. (2007). (Meslekî Eğitim ve Öğretim Sisteminin Güçlendirilmesi Projesi), Çocuk Gelişimi ve Eğitimi, Çocukla İletişim I, Milli Eğitim Bakanlığı, Ankara, http://cygm.meb.gov.tr/modulerprogramlar/kursprogramlari/cocukgelisim/moduller/cocuklailetisim1.pdf Accessed.10.06.2013

Mejia, Luis R.Gomez ve Balkin, David B. (2012). *Management People Performance Change*, Prentice Hall, Pearson Education Inc., USA.

Metin, Hasan. (2011). "Empatik İletişim ve Yönetişim", *Gazi Üniversitesi İletişim Fakültesi İletişim Kuram ve Araştırma Dergisi*, Bahar, Sayı:32, 177-204

Mısırlı, İrfan. (2003). *Genel İletişim İlkeler-Yöntemler-Teknikler*, Detay Yayınları, Ankara.

Mirze S.Kadri, (2010). *İşletme*, Literatür Yayıncılık, Birinci Basım, İstanbul.

Moore, David M. and Dwyer Francis M. (1994). *Visual Literac: A Spectrum of Visual Learning"* Educational Technology Publications Inc., New Jersey.

Mucuk, İsmet. (2008). *Modern İşletmecilik*, Türkmen Kitabevi, 16. Basım, İstanbul.

Mullins L. J. (1996). *Management and Organizational Behaviour*, G.Bretain, Pıtman Publishing, Fourth Edition.

Narula, Uma. (2006). *Handbook of Communication, Models, Perspective, Strategies.* Atlantic Publishers and Distributors, India.

Newstrom, John W and Davis Keith. (2002). *Organizational Behavior*, Boston, Mc Graw Hill Irwin Companies, International Edition, 11 th Edition.

Northose, Peter G. (2010). *Leadership Theory and Practice*, Sage Publications, Inc., Fifth Edition, California.

Oktay, Ercan ve Gül Hasan. (2003). "Çalışanların Duygusal Bağlılıklarının Sağlanmasında Conger Ve Kanungo'nun Karizmatik Lider Özelliklerinin Etkileri Üzerine Karaman Ve Aksaray Emniyet Müdürlüklerinde Yapılan Bir Araştırma" *Selçuk Üniversitesi Sosyal Bilimler Enstitüsü Dergisi*, Sayı:10, 403-428.

Osborn, Richard N. Ve Russ, Marion. (2009). "Contextual Leadership, Transformational Leadership and The Performance Of International İnnovation Seeking Alliances", *The Leadership Quarterly*,Volume: 20, Issue:2, 191-206.

Ömürgönülşen, Mine ve Sevim, Leyla. (2005). " Reddin' in Üç Boyutlu Liderlik Teorisi'nin Liderlik Literatüründeki Yerinin İrdelenmesi ve Ampirik Bir Araştırma" *Celal Bayar Üniversitesi İ.İ.B.F.Yönetim ve Ekonomi Dergisi*, Cilt:12, Sayı:2, 91-103.

Öngör, Y.Akın. (2010). *Benden Sonra Devam*, Alametifarika Reklam Tasarım Yapım Yayın A.Ş., İstanbul.

Özalp, İnan ve Öcal, Hülya. (2000). "Örgütlerde Dönüştürücü (Transformatıonal) Liderlik Yaklaşımı" *Balıkesir Üniversitesi Sosyal Bilimler Enstitüsü Dergisi*, Cilt: 3, Sayı:4, 207-227.

Özbent, Sueda. (2007). "Sınıfta Beden Dili", *Gazi Üniversitesi Gazi Eğitim Fakültesi Dergisi*, Cilt: 27, Sayı: 2, 259-289.

Özdaşlı, Kürşat ve Yücel, Serkan. (2010). "Yöneticiye Bağlılıkta Yöneticiye Güvenin Etkisi: Yapısal Eşitlik Modeli İle Bir Analiz", *Süleyman Demirel Üniversitesi Sosyal Bilimler Enstitüsü Dergisi*, Yıl:2010/1, Sayı:11, 67-83.

Özgen, Ebru. (2003). "İletişim ve Liderlik", *Gazi Üniversitesi İletişim Fakültesi İletişim Kuram ve Araştırma Dergisi*, Bahar, Sayı:18, 99-119.

Özgen, Hüseyin ve Yalçın, Azmi. (2006). "Temel İşletmecilik Bilgisi", Nobel Kitabevi, Adana.

Özkalp, Enver ve Sabuncuoğlu, Zeyyat. (1990). *Örgütlerde Davranış*, 2. Fasikül, Editör: Enver Özkalp, Anadolu Üniversitesi Yayını, Eskişehir.

Özkalp, Enver ve Kırel, Çiğdem. (2004). *Örgütsel Davranış,* Editör: Enver Özkalp, Anadolu Üniversitesi Yayını, 2.Baskı, Eskişehir.

Özmen Fatma ve Sönmez Yeşim. (2007). " Değişim Sürecinde Eğitim Örgütlerinde Değişim Ajanlarının Rolleri" *Fırat Üniversitesi Sosyal Bilimler Dergisi* Cilt: 17, Sayı: 2, 177-198.

Özmutaf, Nezih Metin ve Çelikli, Semra. (2010). "Sivil Toplum Kuruluşlarında İletişim Kalitesini Etkileyen Boyutlar: Ampirik Bir Yaklaşım", Journal of Yaşar University, No:17 Volume:5, 2842–2858.

Özsalmanlı, Ayşe Yıldız. (2005). "Türkiye'de Kamu Yönetiminde Liderlik Ve Lider Yöneticilik" Manas Üniversitesi Sosyal Bilimler Dergisi, Sayı:13, 137-146.

Öztürk, A.Turan. (2008). "Değişen Çağın Aile İşletmelerinde Kurum Kültürünün Yerleştirilmesinde Profesyonel Yöneticilerden Beklentiler", *Çankaya Üniversitesi Fen-Edebiyat Fakültesi Journal of Arts and Sciences,* Sayı: 10 / Aralık 2008, 109-116.

Öztürk, Serdar. (2006). "Türkiye'nin Düzenini İletişim Açısından Okumak" *Mülkiye Dergisi,* Cilt:30, Sayı:253, 29-57.

Öztürk, Azim ve Ünlücan, Doğan. (2001). "Hizmet Sektöründe E-Posta, Telefon ve Yüzyüze İletişim Yöntemlerinin Yönetim Sürecine Etkisi Üzerine, KKTC'de Faaliyet Gösteren İşletmelerde Bir Araştırma" *A Review of Social, Economic & Business Studies,* Vol.1, No.1, Fall, 193-208.

Paksoy, Mahmut. (2002). *Çalışma Ortamında İnsan ve Toplam Kalite Yönetimi,* İstanbul Üniversitesi Yayını, Çantay Kitabevi, İstanbul.

Perry, David K. (2002). *Theory and Research Mass Communication,* Second Edition, Taylor and Francis Publish, New Jersey.

Polat, Soner ve Kırıkkaya Buluş Esma. (2004). Gürültünün Eğitim-Öğretim Ortamına Etkileri, *XIII. Ulusal Eğitim Bilimleri Kurultayı, 6-9 Temmuz 2004 İnönü Üniversitesi, Eğitim Fakültesi, Malatya,* 1-12.

Reed, Lora, L., Cohen, Deborah Vidaver, Colwel Scott R. (2011). "A New Scale to Measure Executive Servant Leadership: Development, Analysis, and Implications for Research", *Journal of Business Ethics,* DOI 10.1007/s10551-010-0729-1,, Springer, Publishes Online: 13 January 2011.

Robbins, Stephen P. And Coulter, Mary. (2012). *Management,* Eleventh Edition, Prentice Hall. USA.

Rosenhauer, Sven. (2007). "Cros-Cultural Business Comunication İntercultural Competence as a Universal Intercultural", Diploma Thesis, Grin Verlag, Germany.

Rowold, Jens ve Heinitz, Kathrin. (2007). "Transformational And Charismatic Leadership: Assessing The Convergent, Divergent And Criterion Validity Of The MLQ and the CKS" *The Leadership Quarterly,* Volume: 18, Issue:2, 121-133.

Sabuncuoğlu, Zeyyat ve Tüz, Melek. (2001). *Örgütsel Psikoloji,* Ezgi Kitabevi, 3. Baskı, Bursa.

Sabuncuoğlu, Zeyyat. (1998). *İşletmelerde Halkla İlişkiler,* 4. Baskı, Ezgi Kitabevi, Bursa.

Safferstone, Mark J. (2007). "Organizational Leadership: Classic Works and Contemporary Perspectives", *Academic Leadership The Online Journal,* Vol:5: Issue:1, Spring. http://www.academicleadership.org/pdf/ALJ_ISSN1533-7812_5_1_158.pdf Accessed.24.09.2013.

Salmış, Ferman. (2011). *Beden Dili, Beden Dilinin Kodları,* Elit Kültür, Türdav Basım ve Yayım Ticaret ve Sanayi A.Ş., İstanbul.

Saraç, Cemal. (2006). "Sözlü İletişim Becerileri Açısından Türk Dili ve Edebiyatı Eğitimi", *Milli Eğitim Üç Aylık Eğitim ve Sosyal Bilimler Dergisi,* Yıl:34, Sayı: 169, Kış Sayısı, 1-16.

Saygınar N.Sinan. (2007). "Hava Sınıf Okulları ve Teknik Eğitim Merkezi Komutanlığında Görev Yapan Okul Yöneticilerinin Öğretimsel Liderlik Davranışları", *Havacılık ve Uzay Teknolojileri Dergisi,* Temmuz, Cilt:3, Sayı:2, Sayı: 67-78.

Serinkan, Celalettin, v.d., (2008). *Liderlik ve Motivasyon Geleneksel ve Güncel Yaklaşımlar,* Editör: Celalettin Serinkan. Nobel Yayın Dağıtım, Ankara.

Simola, Sheldene K., Barling, Julian Barling ve Turner, Nick. (2010). "Transformational Leadership And Leader Moral Orientation: Contrasting An Ethic of Justice And An Ethic Of Care" *The Leadership Quarterly,* Volume: 21, Issue:1, 129-188.

Solmaz, Başak. (2006). "Söylenti ve Dedikodu Yönetimi", *Selçuk Üniversitesi Sosyal Bilimler Enstitüsü Dergisi*, Sayı:16, 563-575.

Sternberga, Robert J., Kaufmanb, James C. ve Pretz, Jean E. (2003). "A Propulsion Model of Creative Leadership", *The Leadership Quarterly*, Vol:14, Issues:4-5, 455-473.

Şahin, Ali. (2004). "Yönetim Kuramları ve Motivasyon İlişkisi", *Selçuk Üniversitesi Sosyal Bilimler Enstitüsü Dergisi*, Sayı:11, 523-547.

Şahin, Ali, Temizel Handan ve Örselli Erhan. (2004). "Bankacılık Sektöründe Çalışan Yöneticilerin Kendi Liderlik Tarzlarını Algılayış Biçimleri İle Çalışanların Yöneticilerinin Liderlik Tarzlarını Algılayış Biçimlerine Yönelik Uygulamalı Bir Çalışma". 3.Ulusal Bilgi, Ekonomi ve Yönetim Kongresi, 25-26 Kasım 2004, Eskişehir. 657-665.

Şafaklı, Okan Veli. (2005). "KKTC'deki Kamu Bankalarında Liderlik Stilleri Üzerine Bir Çalışma", *Doğuş Üniversitesi Dergisi*, Cilt:6, Sayı:1, 132-143.

Şahin, Ali. (2007). Türk Kamu Yönetiminde Yönetsel İletişim ve Bu Konuda Düzenlenen Bir Anket Çalışmasının Sonuçları", *Maliye Dergisi*, Sayı: 152, Ocak-Haziran Sayısı, 81-102.

Şahin, Kübra ve Gül Hasan. (2011). "Bilgi Toplumunda Yeni Bir Liderlik Yaklaşımı Olarak Transformasyonel Liderlik ve Kamu Çalışanlarının Transformasyonel Liderlik Algısı", *Selçuk Üniversitesi Sosyal Bilimler Enstitüsü Dergisi*, Sayı:25, 237-249.

Şimşek, Yücel ve Altınkurt, Yahya. (2009). "Endüstri Meslek Liselerinde Görev Yapan Öğretmenlerin Okul Müdürlerinin İletişim Becerilerine İlişkin Görüşleri", *Akademik Bakış Uluslar arası Hakemli Sosyal Bilimler E-Dergisi*, Sayı:17, Eylül Sayısı, 1-16. http://www.akademikbakis.org

Şimşek M.Şerif, Akgemci, Tahir ve Çelik, Adnan. (2008). *Davranış Bilimlerine Giriş ve Örgütlerde Davranış*, Gazi Kitabevi, 6.Baskı, Ankara.

Taşçı, Deniz ve Eroğlu Erhan. (2007). "Yöneticilerin Kişilik Özellikleri İle Kullandıkları İkna ve Etkileme Taktiklerinin Kullanım Sıklığı Arasındaki İlişkinin Değerlendirilmesi" *Selçuk Üniversitesi Sosyal Bilimler Enstitüsü Dergisi*, Sayı:17, 533-546.

Taşdemir, Erdem. (2009). "Toplumların İdaresinde Liderler ve Yöneticiler" *Gazi Üniversitesi İletişim Fakültesi İletişim Kuram ve Araştırma Dergisi*, Güz, Sayı:29, 149-165.

Taylor, Shelley E., Peplau Letitia Anne, Sears David O. (2010). *Soyal Psikoloji*, Çeviren: Ali Dönmez, 2. Baskı, İmge Kitabevi, Ankara.

Tekin, Selma. (2008). *Sihirli Liderler*, Kum Saati Yayınları, İstanbul.

Tekarslan, Erdal, Kılınç, Taner, Şencan, Hüner ve Baysal A.Can. (2000). *Davranışın Sosyal Psikolojisi*, İ.Ü.İşletme Fakültesi Yayını, İstanbul.

Tengilimoğlu, Dilaver ve Yiğit, Arzu. (2005). " Hastanelerde Liderlik Davranışlarının Personel İş Doyumuna Etkisini Belirlemeye Yönelik Bir Alan Çalışması" *Hacettepe Sağlık İdaresi Dergisi*, Cilt:8, Sayı:3, 374-400.

Tengilimoğlu, Dilaver. (2005). "Hizmet İşletmelerinde Liderlik Davranışları ile İş Doyumu Arasındaki İlişkinin Belirlenmesine Yönelik Bir Araştırma" Ticaret ve Turizm Eğitim Fakültesi Dergisi, Sayı:1, 23-45.

Thomlison, T.Dean. "An Interpersonal Primer With Implications For Public Relations", http://faculty.evansville.edu/dt4/301/primer301.html Accessed 12.11.2011.

Tikici, Mehmet, Demirel, Erkan T., ve Derin, Neslihan. (2005). Bilgi Toplumu'nda Toplam Kalite Liderliği: Elazığ Bankacılık Ve Finans Sektörü Uygulaması" *Fırat Üniversitesi Sosyal Bilimler Dergisi*, Cilt: 15, Sayı: 2, 229-245.

Topaloğlu, Melih ve Koç Hakan. (2003). *Büro Yönetimi Kavramlar ve İlkeler*, Seçkin Yayıncılık, 2. Baskı, Ankara.

Tutar, Hasan ve Altınöz Mehmet. (2003). *Büro Yönetimi ve İletişimi Teknikleri*, Seçkin Yayıncılık, 2. Baskı, Ankara.

Tutar Hasan, Tuzcuoğlu Ferruh, Argun Çiğdem ve Akman Elvettin. (2009). "Dönüştürücü/ Etkileşimci Liderliğin Örgütsel Adanmışlık Üzerine Etkisi: Karşılaştırmalı Bir Çalışma" *Uluslararası Davraz Kongresi*, 24-27 Eylül 2009, Isparta.

Tutar, Hasan. (2003). *Örgütsel İletişim*, Seçkin Yayıncılık, 2003, Ankara.

Ulutaşdemir, Nilgün. (2007). "Engelli Çocuklarda İletişim ve Oyunun Önemi ", *Fırat Sağlık Hizmetleri Dergisi,* Ağustos, Cilt:2, Sayı:5, 36-51.

Usluata, Ayseli. (1994). *İletişim,* İletişim Yayınları, İstanbul.

Uyargil Cavide, Adal Zeki, Ataay İsmail, Acar Ahmet Cevat, Özçelik Oya, Sadullah Ömer, Dündar Gönen, Tüzüner Lale, (2008). *İnsan Kaynakları Yönetimi,* Beta Basım Yayım Dağıtım A.Ş., 3. Baskı, İstanbul.

Uzun, Gizem. (2005). Kadın ve Erkek Yöneticilerin Liderlik Davranışları Arasındaki Farklılıklar ve Bankacılık Sektöründe Uygulama, Çukurova Üniversitesi Sosyal Bilimler Enstitüsü, Yayınlanmamış Yüksek Lisans Tezi.

Ünnü, Nazlı Ayşe Ayyıldız. (2009). " Politik Pazarlamada Pazar Yönlülük ve Otantik Liderliğin Önemi" *Ege Akademik Bakış Dergisi,* 9(4), 1243-1273..

Ünsar, Sinan. (2007). "Liderlik ve Liderlik Davranışı Üzerine Yapılan Bir Çalışma" *Trakya Üniversitesi Sosyal Bilimler Dergisi* Cilt:9, Sayı:2, 1-18.

Vural, Z.Beril Akıncı ve Coşkun, Gül. (2007). *Örgüt Kültürü,* Nobel Yayın Dağıtım, Ankara.

Vural, Gülşen. (1997). "Liderlik ve Hemşirelik" *Cumhuriyet Üniversitesi Hemşirelik Yüksekokulu Dergisi,* Cilt:1, Sayı:1, 15-22.

Walker, Beverly Lloyd ve Walker, Derek. (2011). "Authentic Leadership For 21st Century Project Delivery", *International Journal of Project Management,* Volume:29, Issue:4, 383-395.

Walumbwa Fred O., Wang Peng, Wang Hui, Schaubroeck John, ve Avolio Bruce J. (2010). "Psychological Processes Linking Authentic Leadership To Follower Behaviors", *The Leadership Quarterly* Volume 21, Issue:5, 901-914.

Wang, Hui, Tsui, Anne S. Xin ve Katherine R. (2011): "CEO Leadership Behaviors, Organizational Performance, And Employees' Attitudes, *The Leadership Quarterly* Volume 22, Issue:1, 92–105.

Whitney, Catherine. (2007). *Bütün O Liderler Nereye Gitti?* Çeviren: Fezal Gülfidan, Optimist Yayın Dağıtım, İstanbul.

Whittington, J. Lee, Goodwin,Vicki L., Murray, Brian. (2004). "Transformational Leadership, Goal Difficulty, And Job Design: Independent And İnteractive Effects On Employee Outcomes", *The Leadership Quarterly* Volume 15, Issue:5, 593-606.

Yavuz, Ercan. (2009). "İşgörenlerin Dönüşümcü Liderlik ve Örgütsel Bağlılık İle İlgili Tutumlarına Yönelik Bir Araştırma", *İşletme Araştırmaları Dergisi,* 1/2, 51-69.

Yavuz, Cavit ve Yüce, Gönül. (2010). "Öğretim Elemanlarının İletişim Davranışlarına Yönelik Öğrenci Algı ve Beklentileri (Ordu Üniversitesi Ünye İ.İ.B.F'de Bir Araştırma)", *Gazi Üniversitesi İletişim Fakültesi İletişim Dergisi,* Sayı:30, Bahar Sayısı, 225-240.

Yeloğlu, Hakkı Okan. (2007). "Örgüt, Birey, Grup Bağlamında Yenilik ve Yaratıcılık Tartışmaları", *Ege Akademik Bakış Dergisi,* Sayı:1, Cilt:7, 133-152.

Yılmaz, Ayhan, Ersoy Figen, Argan Metin. (2005). *Perakendecilikte Müşteri İlişkileri ve Yönetimi,* Editör: Yavuz Odabaşı, Anadolu Üniversitesi Eskişehir.

Yılmaz, İdris. (2008). "Sporcu Algıları Çerçevesinde Farklı Spor Branşlarındaki Antrenörlerin Liderlik Davranış Analizleri ve İletişim Beceri Düzeyleri" Gazi Üniversitesi Sağlık Bilimleri Enstitüsü, Yayınlanmamış Doktora Tezi.

Yılmaz, Bülent. (2003). Toplumsal İletişim ve Kütüphane, *Hacettepe Üniversitesi Edebiyat Fakültesi Dergisi,* 2003 / Cilt: 20 / Sayı: 2, 11-29

Yılmaz, Hüseyin ve Karahan Atila. (2010). "Liderlik Davranışı, Örgütsel Yaratıcılık ve İşgören Performansı Arasındaki İlişkilerin İncelenmesi: Uşak'ta Bir Araştırma", *Celal Bayar Üniversitesi İ.İ.B.F.Yönetim ve Ekonomi Dergisi,*Cilt:17, Sayı:2, 145-158

Yiğit, Rana. (2002). "İyi Bir Lider Olmanın Yolları", *Cumhuriyet Üniversitesi Hemşirelik Yüksekokulu Dergisi,* Cilt:6, Sayı:1, 17-21.

Youssef, I.M.Abou. (2005). *Communication Skills,* Center for Advancement of Postgraduate Studies and Research Engineering Sciences, Faculty of Engineering-Cairo University (CAPSCU), Cairo.

Yörük, Durmuş, Dündar, Süleyman ve Topçu, Birol. (2011). "Türkiye'deki Belediye Başkanlarının Liderlik Tarzı ve Liderlik Tarzını Etkileyen Faktörler, *Ege Akademik Bakış*, Cilt: 11, Sayı:1, 103-109.

Yörük, Sinan ve Kocabaş, İbrahim. (2003). "Eğitimde Demokratik Liderlik ve İletişim" *Fırat Üniversitesi Sosyal Bilimler Dergisi*,Cilt:11, Sayı:1, 225-234.

Yüksel, A.Haluk, Fırat Erdoğan, Selçuk Mualla. (2005). *Din Hizmetlerinde İletişim ve Halkla İlişkiler*, Editör: Cemal Tosun, Anadolu Üniversitesi Yayınları, Eskişehir.

Yüksel, Ahmet Haluk ve Bir, Ali Atıf. (2005). *İkna ve Konuşma*, Anadolu Üniversitesi Yayını, 1. Baskı, Eskişehir.

Yüksel, Coşgül. (2002). " Eğitim Senaryosu Üzerine Bazı Düşünceler –Bir Sistemler Yaklaşımı-"*Selçuk İletişim Dergisi*, Temmuz Sayısı, Cilt:2, Sayı:3, 4-16.

Yüksel, İhsan. (2005). "İletişimin İş Tatmini Üzerindeki Etkileri: Bir İşletmede Yapılan Görgül Çalışma", *Doğuş Üniversitesi Dergisi*, 6(2), 291-306.

Index

S. Ünsar, *Leadership and Communication*, Contributions to Management Science,
DOI 10.1007/978-3-319-05248-9, © Springer International Publishing Switzerland 2014